STORMS IN
THE SEA WIND

In his twenty-year career as a journalist, Alam Srinivas, Business Editor, *Outlook*, has worked for premier Indian publications like *The Times of India*, *Businessworld*, *India Today* and *Business Today*. He has focused on investigative pieces exposing corporate corruption and the nexus between big business and politics. Since 1986, he has written dozens of articles on the Reliance group and the various controversies that gripped the Ambani family. He lives in Delhi.

OTHER LOTUS TITLES :

Boman Desai	*A Woman Madly in Love*
Chaman Nahal	*Silent Life: Memoirs of a Writer*
Duff Hart - Davis	*Honorary Tiger: The Life of Billy Arjan Singh*
Frank Simoes	*Frank Unedited*
Frank Simoes	*Frank Simoes' Goa*
Harinder Baweja (ed.)	*Most Wanted: Profiles of Terror*
J.N. Dixit (ed.)	*External Affairs: Cross-Border Relations*
Mallikarjun Mansur Trans. Pt. Rajshekhar Mansur	*Rasa Yatra: My Journey in Music*
M.J. Akbar	*India: The Siege Within*
M.J. Akbar	*Kashmir: Behind the Vale*
M.J. Akbar	*Nehru: The Making of India*
M.J. Akbar	*Riot after Riot*
M.J. Akbar	*The Shade of Swords*
M.J. Akbar	*Byline*
Meghnad Desai	*Nehru's Hero Dilip Kumar: In the Life of India*
Namita Bhandari (ed.)	*India and the World: A Blueprint for Partnership and Growth*
Nayantara Sahgal (ed.)	*Before Freedom: Nehru's Letters to His Sister*
Rohan Gunaratna	*Inside Al Qaeda*
Eric S. Margolis	*War at the Top of the World*
Maj. Gen. Ian Cardozo	*Param Vir: Our Heroes in Battle*
Mushirul Hasan	*India Partitioned. 2 Vols*
Mushirul Hasan	*John Company to the Republic*
Mushirul Hasan	*Knowledge Power and Politics*
Ruskin Bond	*The Green Book*
Saad Bin Jung	*Wild Tales from the Wild*
Satish Jacob	*From Hotel Palestine Baghdad*

FORTHCOMING TITLES :

Dr Verghese Kurien with Gouri Salvi	*I Too Had a Dream: The Life and Times of Verghese Kurian*
Aitzaz Ahsan	*The Indus Saga: From Pataliputra to Pakistan*

AMBANI VS AMBANI
STORMS IN THE SEA WIND

ALAM SRINIVAS

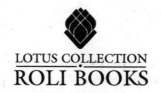

LOTUS COLLECTION
ROLI BOOKS

Lotus Collection

© Alam Srinivas 2005

All rights reserved. No part of this publication
may be reproduced or transmitted, in any form
or by any means, without the prior permission
of the publisher.

First published in 2005
The Lotus Collection
An imprint of
Roli Books Pvt. Ltd.
M-75, G.K. II Market, New Delhi 110 048
Phones: ++91 (011) 2921 2271, 2921 2782
2921 0886, Fax: ++91 (011) 2921 7185
E-mail: roli@vsnl.com
Website: rolibooks.com
Also at
Varanasi, Bangalore, Jaipur

Cover design : Arati Subramanyam
Layout design : Narendra Shahi
Front & Back Cover Photos: courtesy *Outlook*

ISBN: 81-7436-417-X
Rs. 250

Typeset in Fairfield LH Light by Roli Books Pvt. Ltd. and
printed at Syndicate Binders, Noida (UP)

To Rama
who was the only one convinced
that I had a book in me

Contents

Introduction: A New Beginning   ix

Dramatis Personnae   xvi

1	The Cloak-and-Dagger Tale	1
2	A Tale of Two Truths	27
3	Lifting the Veil	60
4	Infocomm or Info-Bomb	85
5	Riding the RIL Tiger	120
6	Anatomy of a Split	149
7	Dhirubhai's Legacy	180
8	The Future of Business Families	211
9	Epilogue: End of an Era	230

Introduction
A New Beginning

'The bubble is about to burst.' For nearly twenty years, at regular intervals, I had heard this comment from insiders in the Reliance group, as well as its numerous enemies. I was myself guilty of reiterating it in discussions and reflecting it in some of the stories that I had written on the Ambani family, which owned the Rs 100,000 crore Reliance empire.

The bubble not only remained intact, it kept growing ever bigger in strength, stature and power. However, events of the past few months – actually, since November 2004 – almost made this prediction come true. It took someone within the family to rock the foundations on which the House of Ambanis was built – both their permanent residence at Mumbai's Sea Wind and their business headquarters at Maker Chambers IV in the city's crowded Nariman Point.

Ever since the patriarch, Dhirubhai Ambani, died in July 2002, there were rumours of tensions between his two sons, Mukesh and Anil. In January 2004, a senior Reliance manager himself confirmed this to me and added that the brothers were on the verge of a split. He promised to provide the details at our next meeting.

I was delighted. This would be my big moment. I could scoop the biggest story in India's corporate history – the owners of India's largest private sector company, Reliance Industries Ltd. (RIL), and the largest group, were about to part ways and divide the pie. (Until then, in a few TV shows, the two brothers had emphasized that all was well between them.)

Alas, my big moment wasn't meant to be. My Reliance source backtracked the next day. At our next meeting, he simply said that there was no truth to what he had told me earlier. I was disappointed by this dishonest U-turn. However, I knew there was something in the air.

My journalistic antennae were up again in mid-2004, when *The Times of India* carried a puzzling piece on its front page. It had no names – either of people or companies or groups; it did not have a byline. But it talked about tensions between brothers, who owned one of the largest business groups in India. It spoke of tensions between the wives of these brothers. In general, it hinted at something spectacular in this group – something like a split. Ordinary readers may not have been able to decipher the secret message; but journalists knew that the *TOI* was referring to the Mumbai-based Reliance group and the two Ambani brothers.

In *Outlook*'s edit meetings, we discussed the *TOI* story. We debated whether we should pursue it and do a larger piece in the magazine. Finally, we let it be; we concluded that unless we could get someone who would say it on record, or unearth some evidence, we would be speculating about it and sound as pointless as the *TOI*. My investigations continued. I kept cajoling all my Reliance sources. (I had several of them as I had been covering the group since 1986 when the corpo-political tussle between Dhirubhai's Reliance and Nusli Wadia's Bombay Dyeing was at its height.) But all in vain.

Then, on 18 November 2004, the Ambani explosion was heard across the country. The previous night, on 17 November, Mukesh gave a detonating sound bite to CNBC-TV 18. He told the TV channel that there were some ownership issues in the Reliance group but 'these are in the private domain, and as far as Reliance is concerned, it is a very, very strong professional company.' The cat was out of the bag. Everyone understood the implication of those words. Mukesh could have ownership issues with only one family member, his younger brother Anil. After all, the two brothers owned the group after their father's death; only they could have issues relating to ownership.

In a subsequent clarification, Mukesh claimed that there were no ownership issues, that they were settled during Dhirubhai's lifetime. But he was sending a clear message: he was the owner, he was the boss, and Reliance was his.

Obviously, Anil could not take that lying down. He decided to go to war. He took to the street armed with dozens of allegations against his elder brother. He behaved as if he had only one priority: to destroy Mukesh and, in the process, demolish the Reliance group as well as himself. He became like a man possessed, who had nothing to lose – and everything to gain. As days progressed, and the battle escalated, one realized that it did not matter to Anil as to who was getting hit and falling by the wayside. He was fighting for his life – and his future.

In his own way, Mukesh retaliated. Armed with his battery of advisors and loyalists, he tried to atomize Anil. It was unlike any other corporate war. It was fierce, violent, cruel, bloodthirsty and savage. No rules applied here: character assassinations, charges of personal and corporate corruption, of political nexus and business blunders were part of this battle.

Anil raised issues of corporate governance, corporate ethics, personal morals, business strategies and basic values against his elder brother. Mukesh let it be known that Anil lacked business acumen, had a playboyish image and was disinterested in family businesses. And there were a host of loyalists, advisors, friends, professionals and aides who were giving their own spin to the events. All this led inexorably to a division of India's Inc's first family, which took place on 18 June 2005.

This book is a blow-by-blow account of the war between Mukesh and Anil. It provides a perspective not only on the fast moving events of the last seven months but also examines the genesis of the differences between the two brothers – how their personalities and later, their spouses, widened the gulf between them. In addition, it is about the mindsets and thought processes that governed the cast of characters – why they did or said what they did, what their motives and objectives were, whether everything was planned and deliberate, and how egos and personality clashes influenced events.

Finally, it is about information that never became public. Most journalists who reported on the Ambanis were allied to one side or the other. For months, what you read or heard were biased versions. The truth was lost; those who were reporting on the issue deliberately left out crucial information. This book is actually an attempt to reveal all the details – sensitive, critical or sensational – that a number of players would not want to become public or known to the other side (even today).

Anil's allegations were, at one level, simple enough. His elder brother had 'used' RIL to finance his personal ambitions; in many ways, RIL – the flagship of the group, the cash cow and the publicly-listed firm with millions of shareholders – had been 'unfairly used' for personal gains. So Anil raised a number of corporate governance issues; he also circulated a 500-page report on it in relevant political, regulatory and corporate quarters. Anil fleshed out how Mukesh was treating the Reliance group like his personal fiefdom and alienating other family members – like himself – from the decision-making process. In addition, investigations pointed out that Mukesh might have changed the group's ownership pattern in his favour, leaving his younger brother in the lurch.

Mukesh too had his problems with Anil. The former saw the younger brother as a non-serious businessman; one who had more time to go to parties, rub shoulders with politicians and middlemen, and move around with celebrities. Anil, according to Mukesh, had the potential to negatively impact the Reliance group because of his impulsive traits. In addition, Anil just did not have the business savvy to run, manage and control such a huge group. So he had to be restrained and restricted in his power and clout. Finally, Anil's decisions – both personal and business – were harming Reliance's interests. His proximity to certain politicians was impacting the future of the group's telecom venture, which was Mukesh's baby. His tendency to announce ambitious projects would squander RIL's cashflows. And his increasing openness in criticizing the elder brother could send the wrong signals to Reliance's investors and impact the scrip prices of group firms.

In the past few months, I have often been asked as to who was right and who wrong. Was Mukesh the initiator of the fight? Or was it Anil's fault? Who was responsible for what happened in Reliance – and the subsequent Ambani split? I believe the problem lay with both sides. I think there were several people who played a role in intensifying the public fight between the Ambani brothers.

Obviously, Mukesh was at fault; he surreptitiously tried to distance his brother from both the ownership of the Reliance group and the decision-making process in the flagship. He may have done it for what he thought were the right reasons and to protect the interests of the group. But he did so without the knowledge of other members, including his mother. Clearly, Mukesh's advisors initiated moves that would push him at the helm of Reliance and make him an unchallenged heir to the throne. Mukesh believed he could take Reliance to new commanding heights, which would make him his father's true son.

Not that Anil was a weakling caught in the midst of a storm unleashed by his elder brother. In a sense, Anil was the initiator of the split. He wanted out so that he could prove that he was a better entrepreneur than Mukesh. Anil wanted a sweetener of an agreement that would enable him to accomplish his goals and further his business ambitions. All that he did was put pressure on Mukesh – from November 2002, when the two sides began closed-door negotiations on how best to divide Reliance between themselves – to get a better deal. Even when the fight became public, Anil's endeavour was to use the media and public pressure to force Mukesh to give in to his demands. The younger brother also used family members – mother and two sisters – to push Mukesh against the wall. It was all about money, power and ego, as far as Anil was concerned.

This book is about that. It is about the internal and external forces that could have ripped apart the Ambani family and imploded the Reliance group. It is about unrelated factors (like the tensions between the wives of the two brothers) that made it impossible for Mukesh and Anil to work together. It is about a family that was gripped by the compulsions to disintegrate.

New Delhi   Alam Srinivas
June 2005

Dramatis Personae

Dhirubhai Ambani

The late patriarch of the Ambani family who built the Reliance group from scratch into India's most powerful business empire within three decades

Kokilaben Ambani

Dhirubhai's traditional wife who never interfered in Reliance affairs; but she had to cajole her sons towards a settlement when they openly fought each other

Mukesh Ambani

The elder sibling – a shy and introverted man who saw himself as the rightful inheritor to his father's legacy and the Ambani empire

Anil Ambani

The younger son who had major ego and personality clashes with Mukesh; in the end, he settled for his pound of flesh

Nita Ambani

Mukesh's conservative wife who suddenly had the urge and the desire to get involved in Reliance's business affairs and became Mukesh's sounding board

Tina Ambani

Anil's glamorous wife whose entry into the Ambani family was resented by almost everyone, including Dhirubhai and Kokilaben

Anand Jain

He has been criticized as a Shakuni by Anil, admired as a die-hard-loyalist and friend by Mukesh, and cherished as a true devotee of the Ambani family by Nita

Manoj Modi

The brawn in Mukesh's coterie, who got things done and also pushed one of the Reliance group companies into a long-drawn-out clash with policy makers

Amitabh Jhunjhunwala

Anil's soft-spoken, smart, suave advisor, who had the ability to outsmart, outmanoeuvre and out-spin anyone else, including journalists

Tony Jesudasan

The earthy yet efficient lobbyist who helped Anil convey his views in the media and in political and bureaucratic circles

K.V. Kamath

The ICICI chief was the mediator who helped the two Ambani brothers smoke the peace pipe; he had political blessings to achieve that objective

P. Chidambaram

The country's finance minister who kept political

opposition against Mukesh on a leash during the entire drama; in fact, he helped the two brothers work out an agreement

Sonia Gandhi

Congress supremo, who had to be wooed by both Mukesh and Anil for political and business reasons

Pramod Mahajan

The former telecom minister, who was accused of being close to Mukesh and who vehemently denied it

Mulayam Singh Yadav

The UP chief minister and leader of the Samajwadi Party's (SP) whose proximity to Anil created bad blood between the two Ambani brothers

Amar Singh

SP's general secretary and a high-profile middleman; although he would have liked to have played a role, he was essentially kept out of the Ambani war

Nikhil Meswani

A cousin of Mukesh and Anil; he switched to Mukesh's side early on and tried to outdo Amitabh in wooing the media

Hital Meswani

Another cousin of the Ambani bothers whose grouse seemed to have been more against his own brother, Nikhil, than against any of the Ambanis; he sided with Mukesh

Balu, or S. Balasubramaniam

An age-old and controversial lobbyist for Dhirubhai, who owed his allegiance to Mukesh

R.K. Mishra

A family friend who tried to act as an honest mediator

Shankar Adwal

Mukesh's chief lobbyist in Delhi; he constantly lamented the fact that the two Ambanis were fighting so openly

Dayanidhi Maran

The telecom minister who went after Reliance, despite the opposition he faced

Prem Chand Gupta

The minister for company affairs who never revealed his true cards in the Ambani poker game and kept changing his stance regularly

Pradip Baijal

The telecom regulator who was seen by his critics as being pro-Ambani, rather pro-Mukesh, and had to keep denying the allegations

Ram Vilas Paswan

The minister for chemicals and fertilizers who was pressured by Anil to play a role; the politician shied away from it

1
The Cloak-and-Dagger Tale

Secret operations are essential in war; upon them the army relies to make its every move.
— *The Art of War* by Sun Tzu

And carry them to an extreme.
— Ambani interpretation

I did the typical journalistic thing that winter morning. From my landline, I made a cold call to Amitabh Jhunjhunwala, a director at Reliance Energy and a close aide of Anil Ambani, to get his reaction on the biggest business story of the year. Just yesterday, on 18 November 2004, the world got to know that the two Ambani brothers were on a warpath. They were fighting to gain control over India's largest business group, the Rs 100,000 crore Reliance empire. And it was expected to be a dramatic corporate spectacle.

The response was mystifying. 'Let's not talk on this line. Let me call you back in five minutes.' It was after a fretful wait of forty-five minutes that my cellphone rang. The screen simply said, 'private number calling'. It was Amitabh.

'What happened? Why didn't you speak then?'

'No, no. I didn't want to speak to you on your landline. This is better.'

'Meaning… Is it easier to tap a landline-to-mobile call than a mobile-to-mobile one?' I joked.

'Yes' was his curt and serious reply.

If this was paranoid, it was nothing compared to what I would learn later. The short and slightly rotund high-flier Tony Jesudasan was behaving oddly. Earlier, he would insist I meet him in his Le Meridien annexe office – he perhaps liked to show off his journalistic connections. Now, his meeting points became less conspicuous and he chose places like Green Park's Barista or Khan Market's Café Turtle. Was it that he did not want people to know whether or where he met me?

In one of our usual exchanges in December 2004, Tony let me in on to a secret. While slipping me one of those numerous, mysterious and controversial notes (on plain A4 sheets) that I had got from several people in the past two months, he said, 'I'm giving you this but my people haven't been able to confirm everything. They're still on the job, but the information is correct. I guarantee it.'

'Your people! I thought you were a one-man army,' I asked a tangential question as usual.

'How do you think I am getting this dirt. I have had to hire detectives to do the underground work.'

'Oh, can you give me their names? Even I need to use them at times. How much do they charge?'

'They cost a bit. They need to travel in Mumbai and to Gujarat. They need to park themselves in small hotels for days and weeks. They need to take people out for drinks to loosen their tongues, or to dance bars to make them talk. Yes, it does cost a lot of money,' revealed Tony.

He went a bit further as I didn't make the mistake of interrupting him.

'Even they (the other camp) have hired detectives to dig dirt on Anil (Ambani) Bhai and me. But they didn't find anything against me…'

Little did he know that a few months later, in March 2005, he would be vilified through an amateurish, but hard-hitting, smear campaign.

In that month, a four-page note was quietly circulated to several journalists through anonymous couriers; as usual the mysterious memo was on a plain piece of paper and unsigned. Although one could always guess who had sent these, it wasn't possible to officially pinpoint the sources. This note, titled 'The Spy As Executive', accused Tony of being a CIA spy with links to both Indian and British intelligence agencies. It alleged that before joining Reliance, he had worked for the Company (the CIA) for many years during his stint at the United States Information Service (USIS) in New Delhi. He had left it 'in the wake of the disintegration of the USSR and the subsequent budget squeeze on the US intelligence outfit.'

The note fleshed out Tony's real work. 'All these years, he flashed the Ambani card to gain access to powerful people in the capital and then facilitate their meetings with either US diplomats in India or with representatives of high-profile US multinationals, like Coca Cola and Citibank… He manages, unhindered, a "dirty" war chest set aside to buy allegiance of media leaders, journalists, bureaucrats and politicians. He has compromised important public institutions.'

It seemed it was easy for him to achieve these objectives, using a mix of 'fist and glove'. Typically, he would use his contacts at several investigating agencies – like the Central Vigilance Commission, Central Bureau of Investigation (CBI) and the Intelligence Bureau (IB) – to dig up damaging information against civil servants. 'He then secures their loyalty on the promise of getting the "files closed",' the note continued.

When the carrot failed to get someone on his side, Tony apparently took the next step. 'Jesudasan is responsible for mounting honey trap operations on a host of senior bureaucrats and their relatives.' The note then went on to mention a few of them. 'Recent reports in the media of three Union ministers being video-taped in embarrassing situations have been traced to his network. A daring attempt to infiltrate a senior cabinet minister's office was defeated only by the direct intervention of the highest quarters in the government... More than a business executive, Jesudasan is emerging as a principal lobbyist and bag man for a clique of politicians actively trying to destabilize the government and bring in a "third front-type" arrangement.' (The third front traces its origins to the United Front regime in the mid-1990s.)

The note ended with a series of questions. 'The question is: does Anil Ambani know that his henchman in Delhi is actually a "taxi" waiting to be flagged down by anyone who'd pay for the ride? Does the government know that Jesudasan may use the Reliance visiting card to enter its premises but he is the agent of a host of US companies, if not the US secret services? Does the government know that he keeps a tab on RAW officers posted abroad under diplomatic cover? And once the Reliance battle is over, where will Jesudasan's valuable database go? In which country sits his highest bidder? Someone in the government must find the answers.'

I knew Tony was a key lobbyist for the Reliance group who, over the past few years, had allied with Anil. I was sure he was involved in extracting confidential information from government's files and passing it on to the Ambanis. It was his job – it was what every lobbyist in the capital did for different business groups. But I doubted if Tony was a spy – he certainly did not have the clout to dislodge or form governments. Only the corporate bosses who hired such lobbyists could do that. Some of the allegations in the above-mentioned note, therefore, were unproven.

When no one tried to answer the questions raised in the note, parliamentarians were roped in. On 30 March 2005, Sugrib Singh, a BJD (Biju Janata Dal) MP in the Lok Sabha, apparently wrote a letter (enclosing the note) to the prime minister and the home minister. Another BJD Lok Sabha member, Prasanna Kumar Patasani, used the note's contents in his letter (dated 30 March 2005) to the prime minister and urged the government to probe the matter. Two other MPs from the same party, Padmanava Behera and Trilochan Kanungo, hurled new allegations at Anil Ambani and his set of advisors based in Delhi and Mumbai.

Behera and Kanungo focused on how Reliance Mutual Fund (RMF), controlled by Anil, was pumping in monies into media organizations to buy their loyalty. Kanungo, in his letter (dated 4 April 2005), said RMF had invested Rs 39.62 crore through various schemes in TV 18, 'which owns the CNBC news channel', and this is the 'largest fund investment in the company.' He added that 'CNBC has been in the forefront of the media campaign against Reliance Industries Ltd chairman, Mr Mukesh Ambani.'

Kanungo also talked about RMF's investment in TV Today, which owns the channels Aaj Tak and Headlines Today. 'TV Today has also, like CNBC, been carrying out an anti-Mukesh Ambani campaign.' Although some of these facts relating to investments were true, the specific charges against the TV channels were baseless.

Fortunately for Anil and Tony, the job was the work of a bunch of amateurs. Sugrib Singh's letter turned out to be an outright fraud. In another letter (dated 28 April 2005), he put it on record that his earlier letter was 'a case of blatant criminal forgery'. He asked for an official enquiry 'to find out who has forged my letterhead and my signature so that other such instances do not take place to the detriment of the House.'

The forged letter was a shoddy piece of work. Singh's first name was spelt as Sugriv – instead of Sugrib – his telephone number was wrong, and the forged letter didn't mention his constituency (Phulbani) as in the original letterhead.

Less than a week after he wrote his 'original' letter on 30 March, Patasani too withdrew his allegations, saying he was 'used by vested interests to make these allegations, a fact, which I deeply regret'. His second letter added: 'When I wrote the (earlier) letter I had no understanding of the fact that the Ambani brothers of Reliance Industries are locked in a bitter battle amongst themselves. Having now been fully briefed on the matter, I wish to disassociate (sic) myself completely from taking sides in any corporate war.'

No prizes for guessing who briefed Patasani on the entire Reliance issue and made the MP change his mind. It was Tony. It was Tony again who traced the MP Sugrib Singh, showed him the letter and asked him why he had written it. But Tony was stunned when Sugrib Singh told him that the letter was forged and was not even on his letterhead. In the case of Behera and Kanungo, Tony found out that they weren't even sitting MPs. They were part of the previous Lok Sabha. That was the end of that controversy.

I also knew that in late 2004, some people who owed allegiance to Mukesh had desperately tried to garner evidence to link Anil Ambani with Bollywood actresses. They couldn't find anything. So they did the next best thing. They spread the rumours through the media. Apparently, when Anil was asked about these, he joked: 'What else can a man want – two of the most beautiful women in India as his friends!' The other camp also wanted to keep a tab on Anil's meetings with politicians and bureaucrats, especially when he was in Delhi. So Anil's advisors – who were still employed by the Reliance group and, hence, technically reported to both Anil and Mukesh – decided they would provide a car and a driver to Anil and not ask him any questions about his schedule. Only Anil would know about his meetings. 'This way, when asked by Mukesh's camp, we could safely say we didn't know where Anil was,' said one of Anil's advisors.

There was more to come. In March 2005, Anil alleged his phones were being tapped. He even wrote letters to the prime minister and the home minister asking them to check this. The contents of the letters were leaked to the media. Anil's advisors too believed that their mobiles were being tapped. 'You know, the other camp has imported some kind of SIM simulator – and they can tap my mobile. I realized this when people told me about the conversations I had had with Anil Bhai in the previous weeks. They knew everything,' said one. A few days later, when I made a routine call to this advisor, I got a recorded message: 'The number you have dialled does not exist...' These guys had gone berserk – hiring detectives, being secretive and taking precautions.

It was so ironical. For two decades, the Ambani family had successfully used the cloak-and-dagger technique to hit out at competitors. Whether it was their bitter and open fight with Nusli Wadia (of Bombay Dyeing) in the 1980s, or the tussle to take over Larsen and Toubro (L&T) in the 1990s, the family had honed its skills in the art of covert operations. Now, the two brothers (Mukesh and Anil) were using the same against each other. Exactly in the same way as their late father, Dhirubhai, had taught them to do against their rivals.

Mukesh and Anil had had their differences for long (*see* Chapter 2). During his lifetime, their father Dhirubhai managed the contrast by giving them different responsibilities. But after his death in July 2002, Mukesh and Anil found it difficult to stick together. In fact, by November 2002, they began secret negotiations – through their advisors and loyalists – to find ways to split the Reliance group and part ways in an amicable fashion. The talks failed as Mukesh's camp was rigid in its position – they wanted to control both the biggies, RIL and Reliance Infocomm, which was obviously not acceptable to Anil. Finally, in November 2004, Mukesh went public with the differences that he had with his younger brother. Once that happened, the two brothers were engaged in an open, public, no-holds-barred smear campaign against each other. Principally, the Ambani war was fought through media.

Take a look at the way the siblings – and their respective loyalists – played the media. Anil was aided by his two generals, Tony and Amitabh. Mukesh had a battery of people fighting on his side – his closest advisor Anand Jain, another close friend Manoj Modi, cousin Nikhil Meswani and professionals such as journalist R.K. Mishra, and lobbyists Tushar Pania and Shankar Adwal. (Mishra, however, denied his role as an active participant and said that he was just helping the two brothers to patch things up since he had known the Ambani family for nearly two decades.)

First, all information would come in the form of mysterious, unsigned notes with sketchy details. As a journalist, there was only one way to cross-check it – at the expense of losing the story. While it would take anyone two-three days to ferret out the facts by talking to independent and government sources and digging out additional details, others would have published it unsubstantiated. Or the details would come from vague e-mail ids: the aliases used were Santa Claus and Bhupinder Singh, among others. Faxes would come from phone numbers that could never be traced to any of the Reliance companies or the group.

The leaks were well timed, almost to perfection. They had to appear at regular intervals to keep media attention focused on the issue. Most importantly, after each plant, the respective camps had to wait for the reaction from the other before firing the next salvo. Typically, Anil's camp would dole out stuff to selected dailies and/or TV channels on a weekend to be published or aired Sunday/Monday. The reaction would come from the other side by Tuesday, which would be covered by almost all the dailies and channels, and Anil would fire his new missile through select publications or channels on a Wednesday. By Wednesday or Thursday morning, the two camps would be ready to talk to weekly magazines (like *India Today* and *Outlook*). *India Today* closes its issue on Wednesdays, so it would have the first right. *Outlook* closes on Thursdays, so it could wait for twenty-four hours.

Therefore, for me, it became a nightmare to write the Ambani stories for *Outlook*. Most of the advisors in the two camps would refuse to take my calls on a Monday or Tuesday. On a Wednesday, they would reluctantly talk to me. This is how the conversation would typically go.

'Alam, sorry, but your deadline is tomorrow, no? So, we will speak tomorrow afternoon.'

'But can you at least send me the documents that you have been giving the dailies?'

'Yes, yes, why not? I'll just prepare something for you. And we will talk tomorrow for sure.'

By this time, I would be chewing my nails, tearing my hair. It was a Wednesday, and typically I would have asked for five pages for the story. And I had no idea what I was going to write. I had no documents, I had not spoken to anyone, the story was embedded somewhere in the brains of the advisors and I had no access to it. More importantly, I did not want to just write whatever they told me at the last minute. I wanted time to study the information, digest it, and apply my mind to give it the right interpretation. But I had no choice. I could only wait.

Thursdays invariably turned out to be nerve-wracking. I

would start calling the advisors from 9.30 a.m. They would take my calls at noon or so. I would ask about the documents. 'They are getting ready. You will get a fax in thirty to forty-five minutes.' What about the briefing? 'First, read the documents. Then we'll talk.' By 2 p.m., I would be desperate. Still no documents, no briefings, no story. So, I would call again. The documents were on their way through the telecom networks, would be their reply. Finally, at 3.30 or so, the fax would start buzzing.

Invariably, I was in for a shock. The first page of the fax would read: '1 of 76 pages'. It took an hour for the entire fax to be transmitted. It was now 4.30 p.m. I had to read the 76 pages (a lot of it would be exclusive information), make sense out of them, and talk to the person who sent it. Then, I would have to ask my colleagues to talk to the other side. Also, if we got time, talk to experts on the issues at hand. And then write some 2000-odd words. Not to mention the briefings I had to give to the designers and the infographist for the article.

Each week, I thought I wouldn't let past events be repeated. Each week, I was proved wrong. That's because newspapers, and even journalists, were handpicked early on by both camps to plant stories; I was not on either list. *The Asian Age* and *The Pioneer* would religiously publish Anil's version. Mukesh's camp too had its well-wishers, especially in the Mumbai bureaus of *The Economic Times* and *Indian Express*. When it came to those of us who were trying to do balanced reporting and get views from both sides, the top priority for both camps was to ensure that their side of the story was printed, howsoever critical the story might be about them.

Here's an example. 'Although I don't agree with it, what I like about *Outlook* is that you are painting both the brothers with the same brush. Like, in your last cover, you said both were taking the 35-lakh shareholders for a ride. You are being direct and saying it without holding back anything. I like it,' Anand Jain, Mukesh's closest advisor, told me on one of my several trips to Mumbai. This wily, seemingly-not-so-suave Marwari knew how to make our tribe happy.

Still, it was Anil, Reliance's public face in dealings with the media for over a decade, who was the savviest of the lot. Once we had a long chat about Mukesh and him fighting the war through the media. Somehow, he opened up and disclosed his cards a bit. This happened in early January 2005, a few days after he had told the TV channel, Aaj Tak, that a deal had been finalized on 28 December 2004 to split the family wealth as well as the operating businesses between the two brothers.

In January, Aaj Tak ran an exclusive – which turned out to be totally wrong – that K.V. Kamath, the ICICI CEO and a close friend of the Ambani family, had brokered a formula to divide the Reliance group's operational assets in a 50:50 ratio between the two brothers, and the family's stake in the group's flagship Reliance Industries Ltd (RIL) in a 30:30:30:10 ratio between mother Kokilaben, Mukesh, Anil, and the two sisters (Dipti and Nina), respectively. Mukesh and his advisors denied any knowledge of the deal. I confronted Anil about the veracity of his claims and asked that if a deal had been struck in December, why was his camp continuing its media leaks to throw fresh mud at Mukesh? Why didn't the public war stop, as is normally the case when warring factions decide to sit at the table and discuss their issues? Didn't that imply that there was no deal at all?

Anil patiently reiterated all the things he had done immediately after the December meeting. According to him, he had not violated the spirit in which such agreements are negotiated. He said he resigned from his two posts (vice chairman and MD) in IPCL, a former public sector unit that had been privatized and was purchased by the Ambanis. He wrote a stinging resignation letter, addressed to his elder brother, attacking Mukesh's aide Anand Jain. In the letter he called Jain the 'Shakuni' who was responsible for the family trouble and said it was demeaning for him to work on the same board where Jain was also a director.

Those were the things that the media played up. But what it did not were a few other things Anil did in the same week (3-9 January 2005).

He issued a press release that went largely unnoticed. Written on the letterhead of RIL, the group's flagship where he was the vice chairman and joint MD, it detailed out his designations in various group companies. Anil's aim here was to claim his right over the parent company, RIL. Once he had that, it would have left the door open for him to walk into any other group company. He was CEO, Reliance Energy, but only at the behest of the parent RIL, which held a substantial stake in the power company and whose board had appointed him. He was not associated with Reliance Capital at all. And, he had resigned from IPCL. So, he was actively involved only in RIL and, more importantly, his RIL posts were his by right.

The IPCL resignation, the letter and the press release served different objectives.

The attack against Jain was a bid to expose Mukesh's key advisor and create a gulf between him and Mukesh. Anil knew perfectly well that his letter would prompt several publications to write profiles on Jain – and some of the dirt would be reported. Once Jain's character became a matter of public discussion, Mukesh might be forced to distance himself from his key advisor. And Jain would be unable to influence the deal-making process. This was exactly what happened, at least partially, with the media going to town about Jain. And, as Anil firmly believed that Jain was the only stumbling block in reaching an agreement with his elder brother, this was a strategic move.

As I found out later, there had been no deal on 28 December 2004, as was being claimed by Anil and his two advisors. But surely a process had begun by then. Kamath was appointed the chief mediator, and it was left to him to find out options on how best to split the group between the two brothers. So now that the split process was on its way, the younger brother wished to clarify that he was not controlling/managing/owning any other group company, except being an integral part of the flagship RIL. What the release did was to help him keep all options open on what companies could actually fall into his lap. He didn't want a situation where it would become logical for him to get the corporate entities that the public thought he was running at that stage. The common perception was that Anil was managing Reliance Energy (but those posts were at the behest of the RIL board that had appointed him) and Reliance Capital (but he was not involved with it in any official capacity). He was on the IPCL board, but then he had quit his two posts there, even though the company's board had still not officially accepted his resignation. In other words, he was not really running anything as a matter of right, so he could be given anything – RIL or Reliance Infocomm.

Despite the fact that there had been no deal in December 2004, Anil tried hard to prove that there was one, merely to put pressure on his elder brother and force him to come to the negotiating table. For example, faced with a situation where Mukesh's camp was denying any agreement in December 2004, Anil's camp leaked information that Anil had met K.V. Kamath in early January 2005, on a Sunday. The purpose: to prove that Kamath, the ICICI CEO, was indeed involved in thrashing out a compromise formula to resolve the Reliance crisis, as had been claimed by Anil's aides while trying to convince the media that the modalities of the split between the brothers had been finalized. By proving several links in the 'real' story, they were hoping people would find their version of the family meeting on 28 December 2004 more truthful than the denials by Mukesh.

What was fascinating to watch was the one-upmanship between the two siblings when it came to meeting senior politicians like the Congress president, Sonia Gandhi, or the finance minister, P. Chidambaram. In one case, both met PC, a long-time family friend, within an hour of each other. Mukesh met Sonia, essentially to make sure the feud wasn't also fought on a political battlefield. After all, there were too many politicians who had traditionally been divided into pro- and anti-Ambani factions for various reasons. Some of them were part of the ruling Congress coalition. The BJP leader, L.K. Advani, say people close to him, was angry with Reliance because of his belief that one of Mukesh's loyalists had helped the former home minister's daughter-in-law, Gauri Advani. (In a press conference that was held much before the Ambani feud became public, Gauri had accused the Advani family of ill-treating her.) Advani had also been wary of the growing corporate clout of the Ambanis.

Clearly, such politicians could use the Ambani battle as an excuse to initiate fresh investigations by government agencies against the Reliance group. With both brothers openly doling out sensitive information against each other – essentially against their own group companies – it would be easy to pressurize the government to take action against the Ambanis. For Mukesh, the only way to stall any such attempts would be to get the Congress supremo on his side.

For Anil, the reason for meeting Sonia was different. He had to dilute the impact of initial stories that hinted that politics had a role to play in the ongoing Reliance rivalry. Ever since the Ambani fight became a matter of public discussion in November 2004, there had been speculation that the genesis of the fight was essentially due to Anil's relations with the Samajwadi Party. The whispers in the corridors of power were that Mukesh wanted to extend control over the entire Reliance empire – and even throw Anil out of the flagship RIL – because the younger brother's political proximity was harming the group's business interests.

The logic was simple. In 2004, Anil became an independent Rajya Sabha member, with support from Uttar Pradesh's Samajwadi Party, at a time when the Congress was at loggerheads with the SP. Mulayam Singh Yadav, the SP leader, hated Sonia. In fact, in May 2004, Mulayam Singh refused to join the UPA coalition, led by the Congress, and openly criticized Sonia.

Anil wanted Sonia to know he wasn't as close to the SP as was commonly perceived. He wanted to dispel the impression that he was currying favours from the SP's government in Uttar Pradesh to set up mega projects. He wished to clarify to the Congress supremo that he had maintained a distance from the SP leader, and his middleman-loyalist, Amar Singh. He didn't want to rub the ruling regime the wrong way. In fact, one of Anil's friends assured me that the younger Ambani ensured that Amar Singh didn't make any comments on the Reliance crisis, except a harmless one-line quote that the mother of the two brothers, Kokilaben, would come up with a solution.

Also, there were several telecom-related cases pending in various departments against Reliance Infocomm. Mukesh had been trying to sort them out, but now believed the UPA (hence, the Congress) was hitting back at his group because of the younger brother's connections with SP and Mulayam Singh. So the rumour went around that Mukesh wanted Anil out of Reliance. It was being said that he met Sonia to clarify that Anil's proximity with the SP had nothing to do with him. In fact, Anil hadn't even told him he was going to become an MP with the SP's help.

There was a problem about Reliance confronting Chidambaram too. The FM was under pressure to investigate Reliance on several fronts. Anil had leaked information about how Reliance Infocomm's debt had been secretly parked with privately-held firms, just like the US-based Enron had been accused of doing. Then there were allegations that money had been siphoned off from the publicly listed RIL to secretly fund other projects and stock trading. Both the charges were worthy of further investigations by government officials. But there was more, something that had the potential to destroy Reliance.

Over a decade ago, an enterprising official in Mumbai's income tax department had unearthed shocking details about hundreds of little-known investment firms that seemed to have close links with the Reliance group. He — and others in the department — painstakingly went through each one of those firms to flesh out their corporate, financial and investment links with two of Reliance public firms, RIL and Reliance Petroleum (which was later merged with RIL). But as this team tried to convince its superiors to act against the Ambanis, it hit a bureaucratic wall – as massive and as destructive as the Tsunamis that struck across Asia last December. (This IT official was so badly shaken that he had the jitters even hinting about his work several years later.)

Some enterprising officer prepared a docket and smuggled it out of the IT office. Somehow, a few years later, in 2000, the papers – hundreds of pages – landed on the desk of Raashid Alvi, the Rajya Sabha MP who was then with the Samajwadi Party and now with the Congress. Alvi promptly went public with the information. Immediately, a whisper campaign started that the papers were fake and had been planted by Reliance's enemies. The media didn't take enough notice of those documents. Alvi wrote to the Securities and Exchange Board of India (SEBI), the stock market watchdog, the Ministry of Company Affairs, the corporate regulator, the then prime minister and the finance minister, the policy caretakers. Nothing happened. Absolutely nothing. For Reliance convinced the officials that the investment companies mentioned in those documents had no links with the Ambanis or their group companies.

It was surprising that the authorities swallowed this logic. For Alvi's papers detailed out how money was flowing out of RPL to hundreds of little-known firms and how the amounts were used to buy shares of another group company, RIL. In some cases, the money was used to buy properties. Now why would RIL give money to these firms? Surprisingly, there was little action taken against the Ambanis. The reasons: in some cases, Reliance promptly complied with the requirements put forward by the income tax department, even while contesting the allegations against the group firms. In other cases, the income tax authorities couldn't find legally binding and foolproof evidence of wrongdoing against Reliance.

But now, after Mukesh claimed in November 2004 that there was no ownership issue in Reliance, another question emerged. Mukesh's friends maintained that he owned and/or controlled the hundreds of investment firms that together held over 34 per cent stake in RIL. These companies, grouped as 'persons acting in concert', were the fronts through which the Ambani family had a complete stranglehold over RIL. Through this network, it controlled the entire group, since the flagship held substantial or majority stakes in other publicly listed firms like IPCL, Reliance Energy and Reliance Capital, as well as unlisted ones like Reliance Infocomm.

But if this was true, Mukesh was faced with a big question. Investigations showed that some of the investment firms in the 'concert' that Mukesh seemed to control were the same as those mentioned in Alvi's papers. Some of the names had changed, but the new entities could be traced back to the old ones. Now how could Mukesh say he controlled these firms when the Ambani family had maintained in the 1990s that they had no links with them? If what Mukesh was saying was true, didn't the government have a legitimate right to reinvestigate Reliance? Mukesh realized this. Therefore, he had to stop the finance ministry from reopening the case. And also persuade the FM not to pursue other charges of corporate governance hurled against him by Anil. Finally, Mukesh won the day, as all the government agencies seemed reluctant to act. Was it another case of Reliance's famed clout at work?

When it came to proclaiming who held the upper hand in this political power play, both brothers claimed victory. On 7 January 2005, Chidambaram made a statement on the Ambani rivalry for the first time. It was innocuous enough; the FM said he met the two from 'time to time', he had advised them to resolve their differences within the four walls of their home, and that the government would not take any action unless it was forced to do so.

Immediately, the Mukesh camp started flashing the V sign. It contended that the FM's comment clearly proved there was no agreement between the two brothers to part ways, as was being claimed by Anil. 'If the FM himself is saying he has advised the two brothers, how can there be a deal?' questioned Jain. He went on to hint that the other camp was lying. 'Maybe, it (Anil's camp) just wants to provide new twists at regular intervals to keep journalists busy. Maybe it's using this as a pressure point.'

Not to be outdone with this logic, Anil's aides asked a string of questions. 'What do you expect the FM to say? Do you expect him to announce there's a deal between the two brothers? Do you know Anil had briefed him about the deal, that's why he made his first public statement?' Amitabh asked me in Anil's presence. Anil was in the same room and had been giving me a background briefing on the modalities of the non-existent split agreement.

Even as our discussions in the second-floor room in Ballard Estate's Reliance Centre touched upon various issues, they invariably came to Chidambaram's comments the previous day. 'Did you realize the implicit threat in it? What the FM was also saying was that you guys better sort out your differences, or the government will have no option but to take some action against Reliance,' said Amitabh. His feeling was that the FM wanted both parties to go public with their agreement and stop the mud slinging.

It has to be said, however, that most of Anil's attempts to drag the government into the Ambani mess did not work. This is best illustrated through a few examples.

On 17 January 2005, I got a desperate call from a TV journalist, whose channel was clearly pro-Anil. 'Alam, have you heard about the role that Paswan is playing in the Ambani drama? Have you heard something? Can you tell me in case there's something to it?' I started following the lead. After all, if Ram Vilas Paswan, the Cabinet minister for chemicals and fertilizers and steel, had anything to do with this fight, it was worth pursuing.

The link became clear to me after a couple of days. There was an IPCL board meeting, scheduled for 20 January. And the former PSU, which was taken over by Reliance, still had two government-nominated directors on its board. The government had a residual stake in IPCL, and the two directors were from

Paswan's ministry. So the minister could easily tilt the pendulum towards one or the other brother by taking sides at the board meeting.

Days before the meeting, Anil had started a new tirade against Jain. He alleged that Mukesh's key aide was making money out of IPCL. This was an attempt to force Paswan's nominees to demand the setting up of an independent committee to look into these charges during the board meeting. If that happened, it would be a big blow to Mukesh and a huge moral victory for Anil. It would achieve the one thing that Anil desperately wanted – distance Jain from Mukesh.

For a long time, Anil had nursed the feeling that he would be able to vibe well with Mukesh only if the latter's advisors, like Jain, could be made to stay away from any talks and negotiations. That a deal could easily be struck, minus Jain. There was one story Anil loved to narrate in private. 'My mother asked me why we couldn't send Jain & Co on a cruise to Alaska to achieve this objective. And when I said the cruise would only be for ten to twelve days, she said we could ask them to do the same cruise three-four times. By the time they come back, we would have finalized a settlement.'

While an Alaska cruise thrice over sounded a bit difficult, Paswan could help him get Jain out of the picture. Unfortunately, at the 20 January IPCL meet, nothing happened. It was a tame affair; the only decision being to ask Anil to reconsider his resignation as the company's vice chairman. And the board also okayed IPCL's third quarter results.

Anil also found himself banging against the wall when it

came to SEBI. He tried to push through two items on his agenda with the market regulator's chairman, G.N. Bajpai. One related to the proposed buy back of shares, announced by RIL, in a bid to prop up its sagging stock price. Since the beginning of the public feud, the scrip had crashed 10-12 per cent. For the company, buying back its own shares from the market at a maximum price of Rs 570 per share, when the price was under Rs 500, was a sure-shot way to force buyers to queue up at the counter. But the younger brother thought the manner in which the buy-back scheme was being implemented was wrong. First, he tried to oppose it at RIL's board meeting on 27 December 2004. He said there were other ways to reward the shareholders, rather than spend a proposed sum of Rs 2999 crore on buying back their shares.

In a presentation to the RIL board, he said the company had thought about buy-back twice earlier – in April 2000 and June 2001. Although no shares were purchased, the principles were settled then. A buy-back had to be at a discount to the market price, not at a premium, as was being suggested now. A buy-back had to reward shareholders in a tax-efficient and investor-friendly fashion, not to stop falling stock prices – as was the case now. A buy-back had to reduce floating stock – that is, to reduce the number of shares that could be, or were being, traded on the stock market. But in the current context, experts were contending that RIL should increase liquidity, or actually issue more shares to induce fresh buying and, hence, boost RIL's scrip price. His conclusions: RIL should address corporate governance and disclosure issues and that would be enough to boost market price. For that would inculcate greater transparency and prevent panic selling of the shares by apprehensive investors.

When that didn't work, and the board agreed to the buy-back, he approached SEBI's Bajpai with the plea that rules had not been followed while taking the decision. SEBI gave an in-principle clearance and only asked for additional details from RIL. And RIL didn't backtrack on the buy-back.

To push through the second item on his agenda, Anil tried to engage SEBI by publicly hinting that all was not above board as far as the price movement of RIL was concerned. The scrip, after witnessing an initial decline in November and December 2004, had subsequently gone back to its original level. 'There's more to this than meets the eye,' he told TV journalists just before walking in for the RIL board meeting, perhaps hinting that the scrip price was being manipulated by interested quarters. His team circulated a set of figures that indicated that the price volatility in RIL scrip was due to increased speculation. Between 1 October 2004 and 12 November 2004 (just days before the tussle between the Ambani brothers became public), delivery of shares constituted 40 per cent of the average trading volumes. The figure dropped down 25 per cent in the period 13 November – 28 December. At the same time, figures for future trades showed a massive increase. All this indicated that it was the speculators who were operating at the RIL counter. Since a higher percentage of the buyers were not asking for deliveries – they didn't want to take physical possession of the shares – their only objective was to possibly talk up the price.

The Mukesh camp talked of a bear cartel that was trying to push down the scrip. The cartel, according to this camp, was controlled by a corporate-political coalition that was desperate to drive down the price, thereby adversely affecting the small shareholders. Obviously, a downward trend in RIL's price movement would benefit Anil's cause as it would prove that his charges of lack of corporate governance and ethics against RIL and Mukesh were being taken seriously by investors.

Like in the case of the buy-back, SEBI didn't react majorly to Anil's charges that the RIL scrip was being manipulated. But, in May 2005, there were hints that a few government agencies may go after Reliance. On 16 May, Prem Chand Gupta, the Minister for Company Affairs, said that he had asked the Registrar of Companies (RoC) to issue notices to the group. Komal Anand, Secretary, Company Affairs, later reiterated this. During that period, SEBI chairman Bajpai told TV channels that the market regulator was looking into complaints that Anil had detailed out in his letter to him.

However, once again, Mukesh came out as a winner. For, soon enough, everyone was changing their tone and tune. In a telephonic conversation in May 2005, Gupta told me: 'In February 2005, Anil met me three times to say some of the files relating to Reliance's investment companies were missing. We found out that all the files were there, and only a few were incomplete. We asked those firms to give details. In May, Anil wrote another letter to the secretary (company affairs) raising fresh issues. 'We have asked the RoC to find out and a report will be submitted soon. But we have to be careful before we act on individual complaints or media reports because Reliance has millions of shareholders... it contributes 3-5 per cent of the country's GDP. We cannot unilaterally act against the Reliance group.' Even the SEBI chairman was basically asked to shut up. For the finance minister P. Chidambaram made a public statement that the government always had the power to intervene in the Ambani affairs, but 'I don't think it's required... I think that they are moving towards a settlement.' That was it. It was clear that there wouldn't be any probe(s) by the Ministry of Company Affairs or SEBI.

Indeed, once the Ambani battle came to an end on 18 June 2005, and the two brothers officially announced the details of a settlement to divide the Reliance empire amongst themselves, Chidambaram publicly stated that the government had stopped all probes against Reliance. According to him, there wasn't any reason to do so as the brothers had called a truce.

But that left a lot of disturbing questions unanswered. Are any company's wrongdoings condoned only because the whistle-blower happened to be a family member who was fighting his brother to demand his slice of the family business pie? Does that change anything? Isn't it imperative for government agencies to investigate allegations hurled by a family member, especially if it involves shareholders' money, loans given to the group by government-owned financial institutions and charges of political favours (as will be revealed later in the book)?

It was an amazing statement by the finance minister. But that was the end of any future investigations against Reliance. Clearly, it was a victory for Mukesh.

2
A Tale of Two Truths

> *All men can see these tactics whereby I conquer, but what none can see is the strategy out of which victory is evolved.*
>
> — The Art of War by Sun Tzu
>
> *Even when they see the strategy in retrospect, the opponents should not be able to do anything about it.*
>
> — Ambani interpretation

There was a time, long ago, when they seemed like a happy family. The father (the late Dhirubhai) was clearly the patriarch, loved and respected by all. Unlike in other business families, the two brothers, Anil and Mukesh, apparently had no problems working with each other. Their two sisters were married into families that did not seem to have anything to do with the Reliance group. The sons-in-law had their own profitable regional businesses, albeit much smaller, but were raking in enough to thrive. All of them (including the sisters who, after their marriages, stayed there only when they and their spouses were in Mumbai) had separate floors in an apartment building in Mumbai – Sea Wind – that was tucked away from the main road and couldn't be seen easily if one drove past it. (When I went searching for it on a friend's Kinetic, I missed it too.)

Unknown to most, also hidden from view were the underlying tensions within India's first business family.

There was only a two-year age gap between the two brothers. But right from their childhood, they were poles apart. Mukesh was always the shy one, even in school. He had very few friends and did not like coming to the forefront. Was it a sense of insecurity, or a general inclination to stay away from crowds, or something deeper? Was it a case of a person who feels comfortable in his small room with his few friends, and senses the power he's wielding from that small space?

Whatever it was the elder brother generally kept away from public life, even after he had grown up and was catapulted into the growing operations of the Reliance group. He was not usually seen in Mumbai's cocktail circuit or social soireés. But he had forged a few close friendships at both school and college. And had kept in touch with these friends for decades. Thus he ended up depending on some people all the time – both personally and in business affairs.

As Mukesh walked into the family business in the early 1980s, he became the builder.

His father was a street fighter. For over a decade, until his first paralytic stroke in 1986, Dhirubhai had fought hard to create a near-monopoly in petrochemicals and ensure that RIL was miles above its competitors. To achieve this, he fought anyone and everyone who crossed his ambitious path. For example, he took on Jinnah's grandson, Nusli Wadia, who had formed an alliance with newspaper baron Ramnath Goenka (proprietor of *Indian Express*) and his editor Arun Shourie, to crush Reliance.

In the mid-1980s, the businesses of both Nusli and Dhirubhai were at stake – dependent on two unknown, hard-to-pronounce petrochemicals, di-methyl terephthalate (DMT) and pure terephthallic acid (PTA). In the early 1980s, Nusli had staked the future of his company, Bombay Dyeing, on DMT, a key ingredient for making polyester that was fast replacing cotton as the cloth for the masses. Now Dhirubhai was challenging his prominence by opting for PTA, a supposedly more-efficient substitute for DMT.

Ambani had to be nipped in the bud. The suave, classy and very British Nusli was fortunate enough to find a few crucial allies in his fight against the uneducated, uncouth and upstart Gujarati trader who was aspiring to become the new polyester king. In fact, one of the books on Dhirubhai – this one was banned though – dubbed him as India's Polyester Prince (*The Polyester Prince: The Rise of Dhirubhai Ambani* by Hamish McDonald).

Goenka ganged up against Dhirubhai because of ego. The story goes that the owner of *Indian Express* was told by friends that Dhirubhai had once remarked that everyone had a price... even Goenka. Whether the story was correct or not, it riled the former freedom fighter. Goenka decided to finish off the budding entrepreneur.

The baron had the right means – his loud, investigative newspaper that invariably attacked politicians and bureaucrats. He also had the services of a soft-spoken and seemingly mild editor who could carry out a vicious, no-holds-barred campaign against Reliance. By then, Shourie had made his name as a great investigating journalist. *Indian Express* had broken a number of sensitive stories putting politicians in the dock. Attacking an unknown businessman was easy meat for this ever-hungry journalist. (When you met Shourie personally, you could hardly hear him. But his pen had the might to attack anyone.)

Helping Goenka and Shourie was a bright intellectual, actually a chartered accountant, who had a penchant for figures and an insight into how corporates cooked their books. Over the next few years, S. Gurumurthy, now the head of Swadeshi Jagran Manch, became a household name in corporate boardrooms. He was hated and admired, criticized and hyped, but no one could ignore him.

Nusli & Co soon realized that their job was much easier than they had thought. The reason: Dhirubhai's flagship, RIL, seemed to have bent so many rules and twisted so many regulations that the government sleuths would easily catch up with the Ambanis in no time. Some of these details only had to appear as front-page news in the *Indian Express*.

Therein started a media campaign the like of which had never been witnessed in the history of independent India. The aim: dig dirt to destroy Dhirubhai. The rule: rely on anyone who's Reliance's enemy.

Dhirubhai survived this virulent attack that became a personal one too (*see* Chapter 7). But the episode taught the late patriarch a few critical lessons. The most important one was that if his group had to survive such onslaughts, the business had to grow so big that no one – politicians, bureaucrats, or even jealous competitors – would dare touch him. Enter Mukesh, who took on the mantle to realize his father's dream. In the 1980s and the 1990s, he was the one who would transform Reliance Industries from being an innovative, rule-bending, loopholes-seeking, influence-peddling, adventurous and nearly-monopolistic company to one that was seen as world-class and professional. One that could compete with the best in the world. All these objectives were nearly achieved – and that too on shop floors and construction sites.

This was the time when Dhirubhai took on difficult projects – the pillars of modern India, pillars that would enable Reliance to stand on its own, whatever might be the opposition. One of these mega projects was the Jamnagar refinery. Finally, when it was completed, it was the world's largest grassroot plant (that is, a refinery set up from scratch), set to global standards, and was among the most efficient and least costly globally. It was also completed in record time. All credit went to Mukesh who, along with his wife Nita, spent days, nights, weeks, months at the site.

No dearth of kudos for this one. He did what they could never teach him in any B-School anyway. For years, the media had believed this myth that Mukesh was an MBA from Stanford B-School. It wasn't the media's fault really, for this untruth was perpetrated at all levels – especially the highest ones. In official documents, in formal CVs, in loan applications, in the company's dealings with Indian and foreign stock exchanges and market regulators, in personal talks and discussions, there was always this one line about Mukesh graduating from Stanford.

It was the Microsoft CEO, Steve Balmer, who blew the

whistle on this one during his trip to India in November 2004. At a business bash organized by CNBC-TV 18, Mukesh sang the praises of the Microsoft chieftain. 'Steve and I were part of the same class at the Stanford University School of Business. Steve went on to configure one of the greatest innovation-led enterprises of all times, Microsoft. I came back to India to help my father build Reliance, virtually from nothing to a $23-billion corporation with global standing today.'

When it was Balmer's turn to talk, he said, 'I want to put in one piece of information that Mukesh left out of his very wonderful and kind introduction.' He then asked for Mukesh's permission ('I hope he won't mind') and put a cat among the pigeons. 'But in our class in Stanford Business School, there were exactly two people who dropped out at the end of the first year, me and Mukesh.' Neither had obtained an official MBA, but both had done reasonably well. (In recent CVs, especially those circulated by Anil's camp, Mukesh is referred to as someone who 'studied at Stanford', as opposed to one who graduated from the university.) Some of those who were present at the seminar contend that Mukesh was visibly shaken. Others say that he didn't show any feelings; Mukesh is not one to show emotions in public. Again, we really don't know Mukesh's mind; actually not too many people do. But his opponents contend Balmer's observation affected him a lot.

Within minutes, Mukesh walked out, only to run into a TV 18 journalist who was waiting to get some innocuous sound bites from him. She told him that they weren't going live on camera, she was just recording him and, hence, he could say whatever he wished to.

His reply was a stunning and public revelation of what

was going on behind the scenes within the Ambani family. It was the first time any of the family members openly admitted there were problems between the brothers. Mukesh said there were ownership issues in the Reliance group but these were in the privatre domain. Days later, he clarified that there were no ownership issues now and that Dhirubhai had resolved them during his lifetime. (Dhirubhai died in July 2002.)

There was only one way to interpret the remarks. What Mukesh was saying was that he was the 'Boss' (in fact, Reliance employees call him that) and that he controlled the group. And his younger brother, Anil, had no say as far as ownership issues were concerned. The remarks pushed the Ambani battle into the public domain. From that moment, nothing would be the same again. The Ambanis' sheen would be lost forever.

But we are digressing a bit and will come back to these issues later. Now back to Mukesh, the Jamnagar refinery, and his role as the self-reliant Reliance Builder.

Jamnagar became the turning point in Reliance's corporate saga. It established the group as India's biggest, after the Tatas. After a few years, when Reliance Petroleum (and its refinery) was merged with RIL, it made RIL the country's largest private sector firm and found a place in the Fortune 500 list. Mukesh had done what his father had dreamt; he had wiped out that one black mark on the group's integrity, the one that had troubled and irked the Ambanis for a long time.

Although a section of the Indian media (including the *Indian Express*) had ridiculed Reliance, flung innumerable charges at it, tried to stall and block all its corporate moves, there was one statement that had left Dhirubhai furious. He vowed he would blot it out forever. This was an article in *The Economist*. In May 1991, *The Economist* published a survey on India, titled 'Caged', with a photograph of a caged tiger on the cover. For most economists, this survey provided the final push for Manmohan Singh to unleash economic reforms in the country. Although the author, Clive Crook, lambasted India for its bureaucratic controls and red-tapism that was strangulating the country's growth, he also attacked corporates like Reliance. He said that RIL had taken advantage of the numerous regulations to build a near-monopolistic empire.

A stung Dhirubhai asked Mukesh to ensure that the world's leading publications never wrote something like that again about the Ambanis. Dhirubhai wanted the world to recognize Reliance as truly world-class and it was a job entrusted to Mukesh. After Jamnagar, the world (including the media, foreign institutional investors and corporates) saw Reliance in a different light. Dhirubhai was in the spotlight for all the right reasons. The continuing criticism back home didn't matter anymore.

In a lot of ways, Jamnagar transformed Mukesh. It made him more confident and whether out of choice or not, it did push him into the public arena. Still shy, he was now seen more often at important public fora. He still had few friends, but now he sometimes threw lavish and grand parties. And he talked more and more to the press. It provided us with a few glimpses of this extremely private man.

But Anil was still the public face of Reliance. Flamboyant, brash and flashy, he was fast turning into a corporate celebrity – seen at the right places, networking constantly, the spokesperson for the group, and the man who was publicly identified with Reliance. Only a handful had met Dhirubhai or Mukesh, but 'everyone' knew Anil – be it in Mumbai, Delhi or New York. It had always been like that. As a child, Anil was the extrovert who loved to mix with people. He just had to be at the centrestage – all the time. It was the same when he joined Reliance.

The first time I met him was in his Mumbai office at Maker Chambers IV when the Reliance group was just venturing into the media sector. Anil was incharge of the newspaper project, *Business and Political Observer*. He was the one briefing the media about it. As soon as I walked into his office, he greeted me as if he had known me for years. He immediately started quoting from a few pieces I had written in the past. What amazed me was that he was quoting lines from articles written years ago – lines that even I had forgotten. The subject turned to the new newspaper. I asked the normal business questions about Reliance taking over a little-circulated journal, *Commerce*, as the entry point into the sector. 'How much have you paid for it? What was the point of buying *Commerce*?' I asked.

'Why should we pay for something that's not making profits. They will pay us for buying it and turning it into an all-India product. It's the best deal that you can make.'

Well, that was quintessential Anil – who could give a spin to anything, who thought he was the ideal dealmaker. But he was more than that. A smooth talker, a convincing and confident face who came across as a guy who was genuinely on your side. He could sell ice to the Eskimos, turn around a controversial story into one that favoured Reliance, sell an idea as if it was a win-win one for both sides although it might not be so. And he was simply one of the best when it came to wooing people onto Reliance's side.

During the height of his tussle with Mukesh, I met him one evening at Reliance Energy's office. I was wearing the new Nike sneakers I had purchased a few days ago. Anil's first remark: 'You went for a run before coming to this meeting?' I was taken aback, but only for a second. For, I knew Anil's penchant for running. He ran several kilometres on most days. A recent cover of *Business Today* had him running with the Taj Hotel in the background.

I said: 'Actually, I am going running after the meeting.'

'Why is that? All studies have proved that evenings are the worst time to run. It's bad for health, you don't get the advantage of breathing fresh oxygen. Don't you know all that?'

I didn't care because I had no intention of going for a run. I meant it as a joke, but Anil took it seriously. He was only trying to be on my side, offering me personal advice as though we were friends. In fact, he thanked me for all the help I had given during the ongoing tussle. As far as I was concerned, I had given none. I was only doing my job talking to both sides to get nearer to the facts.

As long as the brothers' jobs were well defined – Mukesh as the constructor and Anil as the public face – there were few problems between them despite the yawning differences in their personalities. During his lifetime, Dhirubhai had ensured that their paths rarely crossed. Alas, it couldn't last forever, especially after the father's death.

At some personal level, Mukesh and Anil knew each other well. Family friends have told me that you could be in Mumbai one afternoon having an intense business discussion with

Mukesh, say bye and fly down to Delhi, and meet Anil for dinner. And carry on the same conversation as if you were talking to the same person. But such an amazing understanding also tore them apart. For they also knew each other's weaknesses, insecurities, ambitions and mindset.

Once Mukesh overcame some of his insecurities by proving his mettle as a builder, he saw himself as the obvious future leader and visionary of the Reliance group. He saw himself as the natural inheritor to Dhirubhai's legacy. He thought of Anil as a squanderer; one who'd decimate the group with his frivolous and non-serious attitude towards business. Mukesh also felt that Anil didn't have the qualities to be an entrepreneur. For example, in the early 1990s, Anil was given charge of handling Reliance's foray into media. The *Business and Political Observer* (BPO) was the first product that came out of the stable – a daily newspaper that aimed to take on the market leaders, *The Times of India* and *The Economic Times*. But, as subsequent events proved, Anil made a mess of it. The entire strategy was wrong. BPO hired too many senior professionals without assigning any specific responsibilities to them. It became top-heavy and the only objective was to hire journalists at huge salaries and force them to become Ambani loyalists. At the same time, Anil and his set of advisors used the paper to further Reliance's interests. Most of the front-page items in those days were on bureaucratic reshuffles with the pro-Reliance men highlighted as the right people to get the new portfolio. Or it became a tool to target corporate enemies and not-so-friendly competitors. In many cases, the newspaper was used by the Ambanis to demolish politicians who were taking up cudgels against their group. Finally, the newspaper had no credibility and died a natural death after the group had sunk in a few hundred crores of rupees. It also marked the end of Anil's plan to make Reliance a media czar.

Despite setbacks like BPO, he thought of himself as Dhirubhai's real son – one who inherited all the right qualities from his father (*see* Chapter 7). Anil was the networker, he could influence policy making as he was Reliance's public face and interfaced with politicians and bureaucrats, he could raise the enormous amounts that Reliance needed to finance its ambitious, mega projects and, most of all, he was a street fighter like his father. As the Reliance group continued to be rocked by several controversies – be it the L&T takeover fiasco or the exports licence controversy – Anil was the person who managed all the relevant segments like the media, political quarters and institutional investors. As an expert in raising cash for the group, Anil fancied himself as the one responsible for the sustenance of the Reliance juggernaut. Without the cash, what could Mukesh really build? And it was clear that Reliance's future always depended on the group's ability to cajole policy makers to take decisions that would end up helping Reliance. Like his father, Anil was a master at this game. For instance, he was instrumental in Reliance marketing a hundred-year bond to US investors – a unique achievement. Therefore, he thought of himself as the protector. Given all this, Anil felt he – and not Mukesh – was the real inheritor of his father's legacy and empire. It was clear that the relationship between the two brothers was hanging by a thread which could snap one day.

Two events made that possible – sooner than later. Two incidents changed their lives – and, in retrospect, they changed the destiny of the Reliance group, its 35-lakh shareholders, and its several thousand employees. For friends and supporters, it meant they had to choose their allegiance.

Dhirubhai's declining health in the 1990s – he had lost the use of one side of his body due to a paralytic stroke in 1986 – led to Mukesh being chosen as RIL's vice chairman in 1991-92, while Anil was promoted as joint MD. This was the first hint that the elder brother, who joined RIL in 1981, was probably the heir apparent. At that time no one talked about it, as Anil's role was still important (he joined RIL in 1983). But when Mukesh was also annointed vice chairman of Reliance Petroleum (later merged with RIL) in 1993-94 – while Anil was only the MD – the issue became clearer. After this, Mukesh always saw himself as the future group chairman.

The commissioning of the Jamnagar refinery in the late 1990s was the last straw in the tussle between the two siblings. Since it changed Mukesh, it led to increasing strains in the sensitive relationship between the two brothers. It made Mukesh feel that he was really running the show. It also brought him closer to people who thought he should project himself as the real man behind the show, and not let Anil walk away with any glory.

It led to a major makeover for Mukesh. The thin cord of cordiality between Mukesh and Anil was at its most fragile. The only reason it didn't snap was because the father was still alive. But FOM and FOA – friends of Mukesh and those of Anil – were convinced that the brothers would find it difficult to get along from then on. It was only a matter of time.

Away from the boardrooms – in fact, in their bedrooms – another conflict was developing between the Ambani inheritors. An increasing rift between two ladies – Mukesh's wife Nita and Anil's wife Tina. From all accounts, the two women never got along well.

Tina was clearly the glamour girl. A Miss India as a teenager in 1975, a Princess in an international pageant, and a Bollywood actress with her first film, *Des Pardes* (starring Dev Anand). By sixteen, she had everything one could want. More than that, she was among the few women of her time who showed her sense of freedom and individuality. To cite an example, she had an affair with superstar Rajesh Khanna, and they even lived together for a while. Tina never tried to hide it – or play it down.

Anil apparently saw her at a party and, as the story goes, couldn't take his eyes off her. Later, he couldn't take his mind off her either. The obvious happened as the two decided to get married. But they ran into a problem.

The conservative Gujarati Ambani family couldn't accept a glamorous and controversial actress as its bahu. No way could Anil tie the knot with her. In fact, people close to the Ambani family tell stories about how Dhirubhai tried his best to break their alliance. The family even used its clout in the corridors of power to stop Anil, going as far as to get government sleuths to carry out FERA, or foreign exchange-related, raids on Tina. Tina was included in the list of film stars raided for a purpose; it was to send a message that she should step aside. In other words, Tina never became an integral part of the Ambani family. She was always an outsider.

On the other hand, Nita was always the insider. She was the real bahu, the family's First Lady. The reason was simple:

Dhirubhai specifically handpicked her for his elder son. Kokilaben, Dhirubhai's wife, saw her at a Bharatnatyam recital, went back home and told her husband she had found the right match for Mukesh. And that was the end of it. Rather, it was the beginning of what turned out to be a blossoming relationship between Mukesh and Nita.

Let's hear what Nita has to say about it. The story she tells people is that she got a call the day after her dance performance from someone who said he was Dhirubhai Ambani. Thinking it was a crank call, she banged the phone down. The person called again and identified himself as Dhirubhai. Nita joked that if he was Dhirubhai, she was Elizabeth Taylor and banged the phone down again. Obviously, the middle-class woman from Santa Cruz couldn't believe that India's foremost businessman would call her. Dhirubhai, it seems, was relentless. He called again and, this time, Nita's father picked up the phone and realized his daughter's folly. He passed the phone to her and told her to talk properly, as it was, indeed, Dhirubhai on the line. Nita was asked to meet the Ambani patriarch in his office. They talked for about an hour and even as Nita wondered what it was all about, the decision had been taken. She met Mukesh a few times before he proposed to her.

Post-marriage, they fell in love and supported each other's interests. Although she taught at the Sunflower Primary School after marriage, over the years Nita became the sounding board for Mukesh. They talked about most problems and issues, even those concerning the Reliance group. She became Mukesh's friend and guide.

In several interviews, Nita has consistently said she was

never meant to be at home, and confirmed that she was her husband's sounding board. Celebrities such as TV chat show host Simi Grewal, who have known the family for a long time, swear by Nita. She's super charitable, she's golden-hearted, she's the nicest person you'll ever meet. One of the anecdotes surrounding this image is that of Nita's long-time manicurist, whose father had a heart attack one night. Not knowing whom to approach, she called Nita at two in the night. Nita promptly took charge, arranged for a car and the hospital. She bore the entire expense and visited the father at the hospital. But, as Simi says, Nita never talks about such incidents as she's publicity-shy. It seems that in this respect the wife was quite similar to the husband.

After a while, Nita took charge of several things in Mukesh's life. When the family decided to shift to Sea Wind – from Usha Kiran at Carmichael Road – she went to the construction site every day, sat in a shed, and saw that everything went according to schedule. She offered suggestions without being too interfering, and oversaw the details. It became clear to family members that Nita was committed, and made sure things got done in a quiet way.

Her next big project was the development of a township for the workers; this was part of the Jamnagar refinery project. In her own unobtrusive but efficient manner, she took most of the decisions on the site, which was spread over 575 acres and was meant to house over two thousand families.

Post-Jamnagar, Nita helped her husband organize mega events during the latter's term as head of the Young Presidents' Organization. In fact, the YPO became the only forum for the duo to make some long-term friends outside the family and their group. They interacted with other corporate families, went to a few parties together and hung out with their new friends once in a while.

The Dhirubhai Ambani International School was her brainchild. Nita was completely hands-on in the school's affairs; she interviewed each child that was admitted and each teacher who was appointed there. She goes there quite regularly. The school has acquired a prestigious image, with Shah Rukh Khan's and Sachin Tendulkar's children studying there.

Slowly, but steadily, Nita came into the media limelight. She got her friend, Chhaya Momaya, to do her complete makeover. Momaya, who also handled her press relations, gave her a stylized look and advised her on what clothes to wear for different occassions. Momaya also gave her tips on how to behave and interact in high-society circles. After all, Nita had to be transformed from a middle-class woman into one who could rub shoulders with the hip-'n'-happening Mumbai crowd, as also the public.

Thanks to that, one picture that's embedded in public memory is that of Nita in tears at a Rotary meeting in Mumbai, while describing the scenes she saw after the Gujarat earthquake. Three years later, Reliance has funded four prefabricated relief offices in the area, but has pulled out of its proposal to adopt the village Anjar due to differences with the state government. At the same time, there are photographs of Nita who is totally comfortable at Mumbai's glitterati parties.

But what really pushed Nita to newer heights was her work for Mukesh's most ambitious project — the Rs 20,000-crore foray into the telecom sector. Reliance Infocomm would establish Nita as the fourth among equals in the Ambani family. (The hierarchy was Dhirubhai, Kokilaben, Mukesh and Nita.) She would leave both Anil and Tina behind. Nita was responsible for planning Infocomm's sprawling campus in New Bombay, called the Dhirubhai Ambani Knowledge Centre (DAKC). She supervised the entire landscaping and looked at other architectural and interior design details.

Nita also handled Infocomm's marketing. Her's was the last word on the marketing/advertising budget of Rs 300-400 crore a year. Advertising agencies reported to her. She predicted that Infocomm's launch was premature, but still went ahead with the initial 'Dhirubhai ka Sapna' ad campaign and the Dhirubhai Ambani Entrepreneurs' Scheme, both of which bombed. It was this setback that led to the exit of many professionals from Infocomm in those early days.

Her role in Infocomm was perceived as a threat by Anil, who heard rumours that Nita would soon be inducted on RIL's board. To close friends, Anil has commented it was unprofessional of Mukesh to get Nita involved in the group's businesses. 'I have never allowed my wife to do this. I don't even talk to her about business issues. Yes, I will support her peripheral ventures, like the *Harmony* magazine, and go for its launch. But that's it. No further.'

There was another reason for Anil's ire. He knew that Nita disliked Tina. The reasons were obvious enough. Nita was so different from Tina that the two bahus could never click together. One was flashy and loved to be in the public eye. The other had a middle-class mindset and conservative social values. Obviously, there was a clash of culture and style. Tina, the vivacious, bubbly and enthusiastic talker, was a perfect hostess. At her parties, everything was done in style. She knew everyone and could get along with anyone. There was actually nothing common between the two bahus, except that they shared the same surname after marriage. Nita probably saw Tina as a manipulator of men, who had used her charms to woo Anil.

The Tina-Anil relationship also explains why Nita changed her attitude towards Anil. Before Anil's marriage, he lived in the same apartment at Usha Kiran with Nita and Mukesh and all three got along well. But after the Tina affair, Nita was never the same again. People close to them observed how Nita would avoid Tina. She would rarely go to parties organized by the younger daughter-in-law. When she had to go to functions where Tina was also invited, she would ensure there was no interaction. At one of these, Nita entered with her groomer Momaya, and brushed past Tina without showing any recognition. When Nita had to show her face at Tina's *Harmony* show, she made a brief appearance with her mother-in-law Kokilaben.

The distance was visible. And people talked about it in hushed whispers. (One must add that, in recent times, Kokilaben, who was initially wary of Tina and kept her distance from the younger bahu, seems to have accepted Tina as part of the Ambani family. The mother-in-law does show up for most of Tina's events. In fact, the Anil camp contended Kokilaben was concerned about what would happen to the Reliance group in the future. In case something happened to Mukesh, would Nita become the next heir apparent? Or would her children take over? And what would happen to her younger son, Anil? Of course, all these questions were relevant before the Ambani split.)

In the end, the brothers didn't gel. Neither did their wives. The stage was set for a messy and bitter battle.

No one, except the late Dhirubhai, his wife Kokilaben and the four siblings, knows the truth (or part of it) about these issues. None of the living is willing to talk about them. At least, not yet. Dhirubhai was a shrewd businessman. He was street-smart. He probably had the best networking system. He had access to the best information about his industry, domestic and global politics, bureaucracy and future business trends. So, wouldn't he have had information about what was happening in his own backyard, in the apartments located just a few floors below his? (Dhirubhai stayed on the top floor of Sea Wind and, after his death, it has been left vacant.)

Since those who know aren't talking, we'll go by the versions of those who claim they know. No, the father did not know about the estranged relations between Mukesh and Anil, goes one version. But even if this were the case initially, he'd have surely known when Anil had threatened to walk out of Sea Wind in the 1990s. Unhappy with his family's grudge against his marriage to Tina, hassled with Nita's changing attitude towards him and Tina, and apprehensive about his elder brother's concerns about his business acumen, Anil nearly shifted to a new residence. But better sense prevailed. However, the patriarch realized that there were problems between his two sons, and also that his own end was near. He took two decisions to ensure that his sons would stay together. In March 2002, Reliance announced the merger of its two monoliths – RIL that was essentially into petrochemicals, and Reliance Petroleum, which owned the massive refinery that Mukesh and Nita had built.

In April, just a few months before his death on 6 July 2002, Dhirubhai told RIL shareholders at the extraordinary general meeting: 'The merger will enhance RIL's flexibility particularly in the context of its own E&P (exploration and production of oil & gas) and infocom sector initiatives and the government's approach towards hydrocarbon sector reforms, deregulation of marketing of petroleum products and the privatization of public sector enterprises.' Family sources now contend the statement was jargonese to convey the following message: 'The merger will secure Reliance's future by making sure that my two sons will find it impossible to split the group. They now have no choice but to stay together unhappily hereafter.'

After the biggest merger in Indian corporate history, no one would dare split the monolith entity. If his sons decided to do that, institutional investors and domestic financial institutions would oppose it vehemently and derail the thought. And the fortunes of other group firms, Reliance Infocomm and Reliance Energy, were so dependent on RIL that the umbilical cords between the former and the parent would be extremely difficult to cut. His empire was safe. This was his final masterstroke, before the second stroke in May 2002 resulted in his untimely demise.

He had built Reliance at a frenetic pace. He had grown it to a level where his competitors couldn't touch it. Even his sons had no control over the group's destiny. The latter could only try and replicate Dhirubhai's vision: to grow the empire further.

There was one more thing that Dhirubhai did. He did not leave any will.

All that he left as a hint of a will was the deed of partition (dated 31 July 1999) which resulted in a complete partition of the Dhirubhai Hirachand Ambani HUF (Hindu Undivided Family) and severed the joint status of the HUF. This divided the minor assets, owned directly by the family, among the various members. Remember that it didn't change the ownership of the businesses in any way. For, the bulk of ownership in the business entities was through a complex matrix of hundreds of investment firms that legally didn't constitute a part of the HUF. By keeping the situation fluid, Dhirubhai felt no family member would opt out. For that would imply a long-drawn-out court battle to divide the assets. That would also imply that the dark secrets of Reliance would have to come out in the public domain. No member, howsoever frustrated and desperate, would ever do that for it had the potential to sink the group.

His only blunder: he did not realize the extent to which human beings can be driven by desperation. He did not realize that people could do anything when their backs were against the wall, that they could destroy anything – everything – in their immediate vicinity in a bid to survive. He did not realize the destructive power of ego. Indeed, it was a combination of desperation and ego, among other things, that led to the final showdown between Mukesh and Anil.

There's another theory or, shall we say another version, of Dhirubhai's mindset. Due to his bad health he just didn't comprehend the nature of the strained relationship between his two sons. He lived in his own world where the family was happy, content, and together. In the last years of his life, the patriarch lost his magic touch. That's why he did not leave a will. He thought there was no need to. For the brothers would run the businesses together, they would take care of Kokilaben, and the two daughters (and the sons-in-law) had no intentions of trying to grab a chunk of the Reliance pie. In fact, there's a story that when asked by close friends about a will, he dismissed them saying, 'My sons are never going to fight over family assets. They'll always be together.'

That's why he made Mukesh the vice chairman. Dhirubhai's instincts – however unrealistic – told him that his elder son would treat Anil like a son, as happens in most conservative Gujarati families, and never let down his mother. And, at some stage, Anil would sober down, give up his flamboyant lifestyle, and find ways of working together with his brother. The younger one would respect Mukesh and, therefore, find some way of reconciliation despite the tensions. Finally, that's why he acquiesced to the RIL-Reliance Petroleum merger. For, in his mind, there was no reason to keep them separate. If the brothers were going to stay together, the merger was a logical and obvious conclusion. And what better time to do it than during his lifetime.

Whichever version you wish to believe, the truth is that Dhirubhai thought that despite their differences, his two sons would stay together due to family pressure and that from powerful institutional investors and bankers. They would never allow Mukesh and Anil to split.

However, within hours of his death, Mukesh and Anil were squabbling over who should become the new chairperson of RIL. Anil wanted their mother to take over the mantle, for in his view the two brothers were equal in stature and, hence, none of them should get the post. The logic Mukesh gave was that, although he had nothing against it, the move would send the wrong signals to institutional investors and the stock markets. Markets want to see a continuity and, therefore, the logical step would be to let the vice chairman (Mukesh) become the new chairman.

It took them weeks to announce the new name. Mukesh won this round. Anil was peeved.

It wasn't surprising that four months after Dhirubhai's death, in November 2002, the two sides sat together to discuss the modalities of a split in the Reliance group. The brothers had decided enough was enough, it was time to move on, and go their separate ways. It was time to end this tussle. Anil came to the negotiating table with his key aide, Amitabh Jhunjhunwala, who had worked closely with him in Reliance Energy. Mukesh decided he wouldn't attend the discussions, and his closest aide, Anand Jain, would represent him. Unfortunately for all concerned, the talks went nowhere.

Anil felt Anand was not really interested in a settlement. Mukesh's aide thought Anil was asking for the moon. The situation reached a stage when Anil blamed Anand Jain for the tensions with his brother. He blasted Anand for stalling a deal. He thought Anand was a deal breaker, not a deal maker. The only way the issue could get settled was by getting Anand out of the room.

At that stage, it seemed that outsider-insiders like Anand would prove to be the crucial factor in the negotiations between the two Ambanis. Anand was Mukesh's schoolmate. With time, he became Mukesh's 'consumate corporate Man Friday.' AJ was everywhere. He'd finalize a land deal in Delhi one minute, strike another one in Mumbai the second, exult over some critical financial details of RIL the third, and make a crucial decision relating to businesses owned by his immediate family and relatives the fourth.

There can be no denying that he was probably the most powerful manager in the Reliance group. And he was not even an integral part of it. Although he had a few designations – directorship in IPCL and Reliance Infocomm and CEO of Reliance Capital – he did not take home a single paisa as salary. He apparently worked for charity, merely because of his close friendship with Mukesh, and his proximity to Dhirubhai, Nita and Kokilaben. 'AJ's responsible for Mukesh's new image and his transformation from a publicity-shy businessman to one who's now seen quite frequently in public. AJ asked Mukesh to don Armani suits to give him a chic look, advised him to opt for prestigious external posts, like the chairman of the board of directors for the Foundation of the International Federation of Red Cross, and decided which publications and TV channels he should speak to,' says a family friend who has interacted with AJ quite often.

Others say that he's been an image manager for Nita too. Although Momaya did Nita's makeover, it is AJ who gives her strategic advice. For example, sources are sure that AJ was instrumental in Nita's decision to start the Dhirubhai Ambani International School and also get involved with a hospital. (The latter project didn't really take off.) Nita consults AJ on a regular basis, even on highly personal matters. For example, he urged Nita and Mukesh to seriously think about succession and inheritance issues when the younger brother, Anil, had a child quite early. (Nita gave birth to twins after seven to eight years of marriage.)

Three decades ago, the Boss (as Mukesh is called by his employees) and AJ studied together at Mumbai's Hill Grange High School. In 1981, when Mukesh returned from Stanford University, AJ left his family's real estate and transport business in Delhi to move to Mumbai. Anand became the property consultant for Dhirubhai – providing the Ambanis with options, and then executing the deals that they liked. He helped the patriarch purchase several private and official properties. Later, all real estate decisions were approved by AJ. Over time, AJ developed close business links with the Reliance group, through firms owned by his immediate family or his relatives.

A couple of months after the Ambani feud became a public matter in November 2004, I received one of several mysterious notes. It detailed out AJ's profitable business dealings with various Reliance group companies. It seemed the non-salaried, but powerful, Anand was making pots of money out of the Reliance group in other ways. For instance, he was head of the society of Chaitanya Towers, an apartment block in Mumbai's Prabhadevi. Various Reliance group firms owned twenty-five to thirty flats in the society. AJ himself owns a few that he has rented out to Reliance employees. When I asked him about it, he seemed unfazed and blasé.

'The builder of the society was murdered for some reason. The apartments were incomplete. The society members asked me to take over as the head as, according to them, I was the only one who could get the construction going. They knew the murder would make it difficult for them to rope in other builders and also deal with the legal paperwork. So, I did it for them.

'We sold the apartments to Reliance so that the society doesn't get bogged down with debt or anything. And what's wrong with it? They were sold at a discount to market prices. Reliance got a good deal. I have never overcharged Reliance for anything. I can tell you that the flats that I own have been rented out to teachers working in Dhirubhai Ambani International School. Nita Bhabhi told me that the three women were not getting good flats in Mumbai, and I decided to help. Again, what's wrong with it?'

But the incident proved one thing. That AJ was quite a dude in Mumbai's real estate circles. That he had a certain clout. If he could take charge of a project where the builder had been murdered, and complete it, it showed the respect he enjoyed among Mumbai's builders.

My investigations showed that there was more to AJ than just plots and flats. His family controls a string of companies that supply products to Reliance, are distributors for Reliance products, or just provide specific services to Reliance. And AJ seems to be at the centre of all of them. One of those firms is Jai Corp Ltd. It's owned by Anand Jain's family; its executive chairman is his father, J.K. Jain and the MD is his brother, S.P. Jain. Another brother, Virendra, is a director and S.P.'s son, Gaurav, is one of the two additional directors. (The other additional director being S.N. Chaturvedi, a name that will appear regularly in this saga. Chaturvedi's firm audits the accounts of several Reliance group firms, including the secret, shadowy, and sensitive investment companies through which the Ambanis actually control their kingdom.)

GP/GC coils and sheets contributes around 60 per cent of Jai Corp's turnover. But it also manufactures woven sacks and fabrics, which is responsible for a third of the revenues. Guess who's one of the buyer of these sacks? RIL. 'So, what's wrong? Jai Corp is one of the country's leading exporters of woven sacks and it does small business with Reliance too. And the bulk of its turnover comes from galvanized steel products,' explains AJ.

There are other interesting connections as well between Jai Corp and Reliance, or rather between AJ, Jai Corp and the Ambanis. On one Internet site, Jai Corp's headquarters was listed as 807 Embassy Centre, Nariman Point, Mumbai. The office was shared by the then unknown firm, Smart Entrepreneur Solutions Pvt Ltd (formerly Reliance Communications Andaman & Nicobar Pvt Ltd). From its earlier base in Chitrakoot in the Shreeram Mills Premises, Smart Entrepreneur Solutions moved to 806/807 Embassy Centre, Nariman Point, Mumbai on 21 August 2003. In April 2004, it shifted to the Dhirubhai Ambani Knowledge City, which is Reliance Infocomm's nerve centre. Much later, it was revealed that Smart Entrepreneur Solutions played an important role in the Ambani feud. But more about this in a later chapter.

AJ's relatives were also associated with the Reliance empire. Resin Distributors, owned by Anand Jain's indirect family member, is RIL's consignment agent. Polyole Synthetics, owned by the same person, handles the Rs 100 crore business of plastics waste disposal for RIL. Another distantly related family of AJ's handles RIL's exports to Vietnam.

An angry AJ has his explanations ready. 'So, what's wrong with all this? Did you know Resin Distributors is paid the lowest commission in the business? So, it's not making money out of Reliance. As far as Polyole Synthetics is concerned, it was the late Dhirubhai who decided in 1988 that all waste disposal should be handled by a known person, as there were several cases of corruption, and finished products were being taken out of the factories as waste leading to huge losses to RIL. Can you imagine how much money you can make through this route? Dhirubhai insisted that this should stop. Thanks to the decision, waste quantities have come down dramatically in RIL, and are the lowest among all global firms. Do you realize how much RIL has saved since the decision was taken? Finally, exports to Vietnam have given the best net returns to RIL. Once again, RIL is the beneficiary. I have never made money out of Reliance, nor have my family members or relatives. Everything was done to serve RIL's best interests. The other (Anil) camp is just trying to malign my name by talking about these irrelevant issues.'

It's a different matter that while talking to me on the phone, AJ also insisted I should not write about these things. 'I am just a back-room worker. I don't want my name to get into print. I want to stay away from all this. By writing about it, you will only do what the other side wants. Aren't you convinced that I have done nothing wrong? Should I talk to your magazine's owner? He's a good friend and we have known each other for years.' Somehow, I wriggled out of it saying I would have to write about it, but I would make sure his clarification figured prominently in the article. I had no problems doing this for two reasons: it was only fair and that's why I had called him, and because AJ had confirmed a number of issues.

Probably the realization that his name was going to appear in print made him say what he did towards the end of our conversation. AJ may not seem a classy and suave person, but he's smart. And he doesn't always hurl allegations at the other camp. This time though, he seemed to have lost control. He went ballistic and hit out at Anil. 'I don't want to say things, and use the same tactics as Anil's advisors. But do you know who's the biggest consignment agent of RIL? It's someone related to Anil. Did you know Anil is on the board of the company? That's conflict of interest. At least, I am not on the board of any of the companies managed by my family members and relatives. And, if I tell you the number of employees who have been hired in Reliance at the behest of Anil, you'll be amazed. But, as I said, I don't want to play the dirty tricks game.'

AJ's friends told me how Anil wanted to pump in Rs 18 crore to adopt the Mandke Foundation, which runs a hospital. Anil sent an e-mail to his elder brother who, in turn, said the matter required RIL board's approval and, hence, shouldn't be made public. Anil's camp laughed at these charges. The advisors revealed the name and annual income of the consignment agent that AJ had talked about. They maintained the commissions earned were miniscule. Further, they dared AJ to reveal the names of employees who got their jobs because of Anil. 'Let him give names, if he has any. He doesn't,' said one of them. The younger brother's wish to adopt Mandke Foundation was driven by his mother's desire to do so. Dr Mandke was an old and dear friend of Dhirubhai's and, after the doctor's death, the hospital run by the foundation had fallen on bad times. Kokilaben wanted Reliance to help revive the fortunes of the hospital. That's why Anil approached Mukesh.

In this melange of points and counterpoints, the hint of a truth was that Anil ended up disliking all the Boss' (Mukesh's) men. He was bent upon destroying their credibility. Apart from AJ, he trained his guns on Manoj Modi, Mukesh's collegemate. If AJ was the brain behind Mukesh, Manoj was the brawn. The latter was a critical cog in the Boss' success as the great builder. He was the one who ensured that Boss' projects – like the Jamnagar refinery – were completed on time and as per schedule. 'Put him on any construction site and he'll ensure that all deadlines, howsoever unrealistic, are met,' says someone who knows Manoj. More important, he'll cut the best deal for the company. He'll negotiate the best rates. He'll talk to contractors in a language they understand and are comfortable with. He'll push, shove, heave to get things done. In a sense, he's a doer.

To top it all, Manoj is one of the highest income tax payers in Mumbai. Recently, he took a term insurance policy for Rs 100 crore, on which he pays an annual premium of Rs 16 crore. He's a director in Reliance Infocomm, and a number of his relatives allegedly work for the Reliance group. I couldn't talk to Modi about it, but the details are mentioned in the same mysterious note that talks about AJ's reliance on Reliance.

A person like Sandeep Tandon is a clear 'no, no' for Anil. The former deputy director of the Enforcement Directorate, the government agency that investigates foreign exchange irregularities, investigated the Reliance group in the 1980s on shell companies the latter controlled in tax havens like the Isle of Man. These shells were used to control a substantial chunk of RIL's shares, and came under the scanner of the fearsome

Bhure Lal, chief of the Enforcement Directorate at the time. In 1994, Sandeep joined Reliance as group president (taxation) and was responsible for liaisoning with the Central Board of Direct Taxes, Central Board of Excise and Customs, Department of Revenue Intelligence and Department of Company Affairs. His critics think the job was given to him because of one favour that he did for Dhirubhai. Sandeep had initiated FERA raids on Tina Munim, whose possible marriage to Anil was being opposed by the Ambani family.

He too has business links within Reliance. Did you know that Reliance owns a software firm, MoTech Software which, according to its website, 'provides comprehensive technology solutions to businesses, partnering with its customers in their endeavour to effectively compete in today's global market place.' Whatever that means. With offices in the US, Europe, Japan and India, MoTech is promoted by RIL. Its MD is Annu Tandon who, says her CV on the company's website, was the executive director of the Observer Group of Publications (owned by Reliance). She's also a corporate consultant to the Reliance group. Incidentally, she is Sandeep's wife.

Finally, Anil's hate list includes the Meswani brothers, Nikhil and Hital. They're the sons of the late Rasikbhai, who was probably the closest partner Dhirubhai ever had. While Dhirubhai focused on manufacturing and operations, Rasikbhai looked after the important liaison work in Delhi. For any business group, political and bureaucratic networking was crucial and, therefore, the Ambani patriarch came to respect and trust the senior Meswani. After Rasikbhai's death sometime in the 1980s, Dhirubhai decided he couldn't let down his nephews. So, he inducted both Nikhil and Hital on

RIL's board, even though they were quite young then. Nikhil joined in 1986 when he was twenty-first and Hital in 1995 at twenty-six. Today, Nikhil does his father's job and, in recent times, had become Mukesh's chief spokesperson on family-related issues. Hital, an engineer by profession, looks after the day-to-day operations of the Jamnagar refinery.

Anil's grouse against the Meswanis is that the two cousins had openly sided with Mukesh. In fact, the younger Ambani believes that the Meswanis have been wooed to the other camp. For example, Anil was convinced that Nikhil and Hital's combined holdings in RIL were higher than his. Although one doesn't know for sure, Mukesh and Anil directly owned 2.5 per cent stake each, with mother Kokilaben owning 18 lakh shares. Most of the family stake (of nearly 50 per cent) was held through the Petroleum Trust (12 per cent) or through hundreds of investment firms (34.04 per cent). But the Meswanis together were believed to own 7 per cent in RIL. When asked, Nikhil gives a convoluted answer: 'Why don't you check the public registry and find out how much we own.' When asked to say yes or no to owning shares in RIL, he laughed.

Anil didn't find it funny. He blamed Mukesh and all his men for not being able to reach a compromise on splitting the Reliance group. When he was pushed a bit more, he decided to go to war. (While fighting, he took a few lessons out of Sun Tzu's *The Art of War*.)

3
Lifting the Veil

The general who wins the battle makes many calculations in his temple before the battle is fought.

— The Art of War by Sun Tzu

Don't just make calculations; wrest the territory before the battle begins.

— Ambani interpretation

Across the globe, there are certain nondescript addresses that are the real business investment hubs. It's through these select – often single-room – offices, hundreds of them, that corporate czars wield control over their business empires. These are the actual seats of money power.

In these offices, unknown and faceless men – they're most often men – pore over thousands of pages of financial accounts each day. During office hours, they just keep making entries. These entries are decisive. For, through their sleight of hand, they send thousands of crores of rupees from one company to another, transfer huge and valuable holdings in publicly listed firms, and decide who the real corporate owners are. A friend of mine described these operations as 'Kafkaesque and surreal'.

The names of these investment entities tend to follow a certain pattern. One accountant may like rivers, so he will give names such as Ganga, Yamuna, Saraswati and Godavari to these firms. Another may like flowers – so his table would be full of balance sheets of Rose, Sunflower and Lily. A third may like mountains and opt for Everest, Nanda Devi and K2. The truth is that the finances of these firms are even more esoteric than their names. And secrecy is the key. Hide-and-lie is the motto here.

Virtually all businessmen follow this practice. They set up hundreds of these shell firms, or benamis as they are called in India, to protect themselves from takeover tycoons, from prying eyes of the government, from the public at large. In countries like India, where tax rates are high, these firms enable promoters to hide their personal wealth and juggle figures to legitimately reduce taxes. But more important, the dud entities help the owners to hide ownership. No outsider can ever know the names of individuals or firms that actually control a business group.

On rare occasions, the veil of secrecy is lifted off these addresses. It could happen during a corporate battle when investigators criss-cross the world to unearth truths about ownership. Or during a takeover tussle when the predator wants to know certain facts. Or, as in the case of the Ambanis, it could happen during a bitter feud between family members.

84-A, Mittal Court in Mumbai's Nariman Point is one such address. Through dozens of firms headquartered in this office, the Ambani family controlled its Rs 100,000-crore group.

It's ironical that the Ambanis chose this address as their secret base. For, the B-wing of Mittal Court is the headquarters of the stock market regulator, the SEBI. While in one wing of the building, accountants were scribbling figures to conceal, in the other, SEBI sleuths were busy enforcing greater transparency in corporates. While one wing was helping big business, the other was apparently upholding the rights of the small investors. Unfortunately, SEBI had little idea of what was happening in 84-A, Mittal Court. But the market watchdog wasn't the only one. Anil contends that he too knew nothing about Mittal Court. What was happening there? Why did Anil want to know about it? Did it concern SEBI?

Let's start at the beginning, when this dark and dingy, yet dazzling, underbelly of the Reliance group was first exposed to the public eye. In 2000, a little-known MP was walking around in Delhi with a dossier that very few could comprehend. It contained Excel charts, flow charts and pages and pages of income tax documents filed by hundreds of firms one hadn't heard of. As an explanatory introduction, there were, however, a few pages mentioning a series of financial irregularities against the Reliance group. No one gave the MP, Raashid Alvi, or his set of documents a second look. Not the media, not the public. Even Reliance looked the other way, except for running a whisper campaign questioning the authenticity of the documents.

I did look at the documents, however, for I realized the information was the result of a detailed investigation by

Mumbai's income tax department. I figured it would provide an insight into the highly classified corporate character of India's top company. It may have been smuggled out of the IT office by a competitor of the Ambanis, but as long as the information was good, that didn't matter.

Alvi's papers disclosed how huge sums from publicly listed companies like RIL and Reliance Petroleum (before its merger with RIL) were routed, re-routed, redirected again for different purposes through a string of companies. He listed 251 investment firms used by the Reliance group in the 1990s for this purpose. The monies were used to purchase scrips of group companies, invest in forthcoming issues (equity or debentures) of group entities, buy properties, do whatever had to be done secretively. While most Indian business groups do the same, it's done in a surreptitious manner. So, when such details do trickle out, it shocks people that there are several aspects of publicly listed companies that are completely hidden. It also scares shareholders that the so-called professionally managed groups operate in such a non-transparent environment.

Of course, it's illegal when privately held companies are used to evade taxes. It's also wrong if promoters use the investment firms to manipulate the stock prices of their publicly listed firms. It's also dishonest when owners use the little-known firms to take out money – to serve their selfish and petty interests – from companies that are listed on the stock exchanges. However, it is nearly impossible for investigating agencies to prove such charges in court.

But the ultimate aim of owning hundreds of investment firms is to retain complete control of the group through a complex system of holdings and cross-holdings. In case of Reliance, this was carried to a bizarre extreme. Money was doled out through several channels. It was given as interest-bearing loans, interest-free loans, advances for certain services or products, application money for buying debentures, or whatever was legally permissible under the law. Innovative ways were designed to transfer money to where it was required, when it was required and for the specific purpose that it was required. And Reliance did it on a grander scale than any other company.

Since it would be impossible to reconstruct and reveal the financial details and complexity involving over 250 firms that were owned and/or controlled by the Reliance group in the mid-1990s, I shall illustrate it through just a few examples. But these will be enough to give an idea of the shadowy financial world of Reliance, and their Indian promoters.

Krishna Associates, a partnership firm, came into existence in October 1994. Its three partners included Reliance Petroleum (98 per cent stake), Amitabh Jhunjhunwala (1 per cent) and Shyam Sundar Mittal (1 per cent). None of the owners contributed any money for their stakes. In effect, to begin with, Krishna Associates was a dud with no money.

Documents showed that, within weeks, Krishna Associates received Rs 600 crore as interest-free 'advance' from CPPL Project Services. Who owned CPPL? It was the same Amitabh and Mittal combine, with a stake of 1 per cent each. This time, the bulk of the equity, or 98 per cent, was owned by another Ambani firm, Reliance Industrial & Infrastructure Ltd. Why did CPPL provide such a huge sum to

Krishna Associates? The chain of money flows now becomes quite complex and seems to serve just one purpose – to hide the identity of the original lender as well as the purpose for which the money was used. In September 1994, Reliance Petroleum, which raised huge amounts through a public issue to finance the Jamnagar refinery project and was the main owner of Krishna Associates, asked one of its sister concerns, Reliance Industrial & Infrastructure Ltd, the promoter of CPPL, to supply construction equipment worth Rs 220 crore. However, Reliance Industrial & Infrastructure Ltd subcontracted the job to its subsidiary, CPPL. So, Reliance Petroleum, the contractor, agreed to pay over a third of the original contract amount, or Rs 82.50 crore, to CPPL. But, CPPL further assigned the work to Krishna Associates, and asked Reliance Petroleum to pay the money directly to the new sub-subcontractor. For some odd reason, Krishna Associates was paid Rs 600 crore. But the money was not directly paid by Reliance Petroleum. Instead, Reliance Petroleum asked another of its sister concerns, Reliance Project Services, to transfer the amount to Krishna Associates.

What does Krishna Associates do? What kind of services does it provide? Did Krishna Associates provide Reliance Petroleum with the construction equipment that was needed for the Jamnagar refinery? Going by the inventory register of Krishna Associates for 1994-95, one finds it was only a stock trader, actually more a buyer of scrips of Reliance Capital and RIL. The day it opened shop, it bought 6 lakh shares of Reliance Capital from one Suresh K. Jajoo. Within a week, it owned lakhs of RIL shares; since RIL was quoting at over Rs 400 a share, Krishna Associates was obviously spending crores of rupees every day. To be fair, I should mention there were other scrips also that Krishna Associates traded in; one of these being Punjab Communication.

Now, we get into tricky territory. If it could be proved that monies were flowing from one Ambani-owned firm to another to buy shares of listed group firms, it would be a clear case of insider trading. As defined by current laws, insider trading implies transactions where individuals and companies use inside information to buy or sell shares and they know in advance how the scrip price will move because of the information they possess. In the above case, if RIL and Krishna Associates had the same, or closely linked, owners, there could be a case for insider trading. But Reliance wasn't hauled up in this or other similar cases because India didn't have any insider trading laws when the transactions took place. Even when Alvi raised this issue with SEBI, he was told that the market regulator couldn't investigate these cases as they predated the country's insider trading laws.

Interestingly, some of the sellers of the RIL and Reliance Capital shares to Krishna Associates were companies/individuals who were quite close to the Ambanis. Reliance Petroleum was one of the sellers. Manoj Modi sold some too. Several transactions were with Jayant Modi & Co, one of the largest brokerage houses in Mumbai. Jayant Modi is related to none other than Manoj. Another seller was Virendra Jain, who is related to Anand Jain.

In December 1997, the income tax authorities issued a show cause notice to Reliance Petroleum questioning these money and stock transactions. The company's reply was categorical. 'In the said letter you have further referred to the funds movement from us to CPPL Projects and then to Krishna Associates. You have also referred to the purchase of shares by Krishna Associates with the help of funds given by us. In view of the various factors mentioned by you in your letter, you proposed to disallow loss of Rs 2636.65 lakh.'

What the income tax department said was that Reliance Petroleum had engineered losses through transactions with firms owned by the Ambanis and funds provided by Reliance group entities. Obviously, the price(s) at which Reliance Petroleum had purchased the shares was higher than the sale price to Krishna Associates. Therefore, IT officials felt that since the shares were sold by one group company to another, it was not a genuine transaction and the only purpose was to effect losses that would help Reliance Petroleum to save on income tax.

How did Reliance Petroleum defend itself?

'We strongly deny the above allegation that the funds for the purchase of shares have been provided by us. We further submit that the availability of funds to the said firm by us does not in any manner affect the claim of loss.' Reliance Petroleum was going to fight back, it would contest the claim and set the record right. But that didn't happen. 'However, with a view to buy peace and to avoid litigation we have offered an amount of Rs 25,12,55,676 u/s 64 of the Finance Act 1997 and the tax payable on the said income has been duly paid… In view of the above, you are requested not to include the income of Rs 25,12,55,676 while computing the total income.' Reliance Petroleum decided to back off, pay the requisite tax and agree with the income tax authorities that the loss on account of sale of RIL and Reliance Capital shares should not be included in its books. However, this did not mean that it was guilty in the strictly legal sense.

Somnath Syndicate was another firm that came into existence the same day as Krishna Associates. (Both the offices were at 37, Sheela Apartments on Mumbai's Bhulabhai Desai Road.) However, its partners' list had just one minor difference. Instead of Reliance Petroleum, it was RIL that owned 98 per cent stake in it. The other two partners were the same —Amitabh and Mittal with holdings of 1 per cent each. Its balance sheet (1994-95) showed that none of the partners had contributed any money towards its share capital. But Somnath Syndicate received nearly Rs 300 crore as 'unsecured loans' from Reliance Petroproducts which, in turn, got a slightly higher amount – again as unsecured loans – from RIL. Somnath Syndicate too invested the money in purchasing shares of Reliance group companies. Once again, income tax officials felt the company was created to divert funds and reduce the tax liability of RIL. RIL's purchase price(s) was higher than its sale price to Somnath Syndicate, resulting in losses for the former.

Again, RIL denied the allegations. 'The above allegations are based on conjectures and surmises and are without any evidence. We deny that our income has been diverted to the said firm (Somnath Syndicate).' RIL went on to mention that it had directly given loans (over Rs 60 crore) to Somnath Syndicate, and the latter had paid interest on it. The interest income was duly included in RIL's profit and loss account. Therefore, there was no evasion, no diversion.

Somnath Syndicate toed the same line of defence, and even went a little further. It challenged the income tax department's contention that since the partners had not brought in money, the company was incapable of carrying on any business. 'It is an accepted position in law and in practice that all the partners do not contribute the capital. Some partners may contribute capital while others may provide services to the firm and work for the promotion of the business of the firm. It is also common in practice that the partner may provide funds either by way of capital or by way of current account or by way of loan.' That is why RIL directly provided an unsecured loan of Rs 63 crore to Somnath Syndicate.

RIL and Somnath Syndicate were probably right, but that's for the authorities to decide. My intention is only to flesh out the world of investment firms, how money weaves in and out of them, and how they're meant to protect the promoter who either doesn't wish to own shares directly, or can't do so openly.

Let's now turn our attention to other kinds of dealings. In the latter half of the 1990s, one of the companies housed at 84-A, Mittal Court, Nariman Point, was Sandoz Textiles & Trading. It was the owner of RPL House in Ballard Estate, Mumbai, and rented out the 36,351 sq ft property. (The name of the building has been changed to Reliance Centre and it now houses the offices of Reliance Energy.) Nothing wrong with that except that the income tax assessment (for 1996-97) found interesting facts about Sandoz Textiles. The first three floors (ground, first and second) were leased out to Suraksha Tradecom, and the top two (third and fourth) to Divya Syntex. Both tenants paid a monthly rental of Rs 40,000 per floor and Sandoz Textiles didn't insist on any security deposit. And this in a city like Mumbai, where 'pugrees' can be killing and deposits huge.

Probably, Sandoz Textiles was doing a favour to the two fledgling firms.

But the income tax officials found that both Suraksha Tradecom and Divya Syntex in turn leased out the entire property to RIL and Reliance Petroleum. And what were the latter paying them? A monthly rental of Rs 1,36,200 to Suraksha Tradecom for each floor, and Rs 1,32,420 per floor to Divya Syntex. More importantly, RIL gave a security deposit of nearly Rs 19 crore per floor to Suraksha Tradecom and Reliance Petroleum paid just over Rs 18 crore per floor to Divya Syntex.

Here's what the income tax department noted in its assessment order on Sandoz Textiles. 'It is interesting to note that the assessee gave the property on lease to two concerns namely Suraksha Tradecom and Divya Syntex at an abysmally low rent of Rs 40,000 per month per floor without accepting any security deposit, whereas the tenants gave the same property on further lease to RIL and RPL (Reliance Petroleum) at a substantially higher rent besides accepting an interest-free deposit of over Rs 100 crore. The assessee acquired the property "RPL House" in 1989 and since then it has been in the business of letting out the property to several tenants... Whereas the tenants namely Suraksha and Divya are novice (sic) to the business of giving properties on lease.

'The assessee company has very capable and eminent persons on its board of directors viz, Shri D.L. Sheth, a consultant of RIL for the past several years, Shri M.F. Sheth, who had long association with RIL having worked as general manager before his retirement, Shri J.B. Dholakia, presently working with RIL as a senior executive, besides Shri Devesh Vasavada, a chartered accountant having vast experience. It is incomprehensible how such senior and experienced people could get only Rs 40,000 per month per floor as rent without any security deposit as against four times the rent besides huge security deposit obtained by the tenants, which has people of no significance on its board of directors. For example, at the relevant time, Suraksha Tradecom had Shri A. Subramanian and Shri P.V. Menon as its directors. It had paid total salary of Rs 25,676 during the whole year indicating that it did not employ any person having any business acumen who could have negotiated such a deal with companies like RIL and RPL. Even the directors were not known to have such an acumen to clinch a deal of that magnitude.' However, the income tax officials couldn't make much headway in this matter because, on paper, there was nothing wrong with the property deals. The government sleuths could only raise a few doubts, but couldn't take any strict legal action.

Looking at the funds utilization of various shell companies owned and/or controlled by the Ambanis in the mid-1990s provides better insights into this money game. Cube Investments received money from RIL and used it to pay up the share application money to buy shares of Global Trust Bank. It got huge amounts from Chandragupta Traders and used it to buy shares and property. It got money from Ornamental Trading Enterprises and used it to purchase shares. All the firms mentioned here, except Global Trust Bank, are part of the Reliance network.

Riyaz Trading received money from Virendra Jain, Anand Jain's brother, and used it to either buy RIL shares or make payments on behalf of Lavanya Holdings, another firm linked to Reliance, to entities like Jogiya Traders, Vatayan Synthetics and Aavaran Textiles. Saumya Finance & Leasing received money from RIL to buy shares of Global Trust Bank. It got money from V.B. Roongta, who has done a number of transactions in the RIL scrip, and bought shares and made payments at the behest of Lavanya Holdings to Silkina Trading. All the firms, apart from Global Trust Bank, mentioned here were linked to the Ambanis.

The case of Silvasa Industries, formerly Reliance Filaments, is also curious. The company issued fully convertible debentures (face value: Rs 100, interest: 18 per cent) and raised Rs 300 crore through private placement. All the money came from RIL, and the allotment letters were issued in March 1994. The funds were almost instantly advanced by Silvasa Industries to forty companies by way of debenture application money in the latter.

Look at some of the issues involved in these transactions. If a company issues debentures, convertible or otherwise, it has to pay a specified annual interest on them. But Silvasa Industries did not pay any interest to RIL – although the debentures it issued to RIL in March 1994 bore a rate of 18 per cent. As of 31 March 1995, even the forty entities had not paid any interest to Silvasa Industries. They sat on the application money and did not issue any debentures to Silvasa Industries as of 31 March 1995. Finally, in 1995-96, Silvasa Industries recovered the money from the forty firms, but the interest that the latter paid was only for the period beginning 1 April 1995 until the time of the repayment.

All the transactions mentioned in this chapter till now are a case of putting the money in the right place at the right time. It is about making sure that promoters' control over the group remains intact. For these are the firms that are also used to hold promoters' holdings, and to transfer money to other firms for financial reasons. But, at the end of the day, all these are merely entries. Money comes, it goes after a while. Shares are purchased, then sold at some point in time. The entire exercise is to save on tax, to hide matters, to keep everyone confused. Except one person: the promoter. And it is rare when authorities are able to put a promoter in the dock on such issues.

But how do promoters – and those faceless accountants – manage to retain control over these hundreds of firms? How do they ensure that no one can walk away with the promoters' holdings? How do they secure the owners' rights in perpetuity?

The first trick in this financial art is to prepare a system of linkages between all these companies. This, unlike what people usually think, is not a web. The linkages are unlike a pyramidal structure, where a few firms at the top have holdings in several dozens down the line and, finally, the second layer companies have holdings in the publicly-listed businesses. Therefore, it's not as if one can tinker with the holding pattern of firms at the top and change ownership down the line.

It is a matrix that not too many can comprehend. If one wants to change the ownership, one has to dismantle the original and create a new one. In fact, it has a lot of similarities with the movie *Matrix*. Like in the movie, the architect(s) of the investment matrix can only change things by building new versions, but only if he/they is/are allowed to do so by the owners. And only if the promoter decides that the existing financial software is not working to his satisfaction. In general, the investment matrix needs to go through various versions. It needs to be refined, rejigged, redesigned to accommodate any changes in existing laws, corporate structures or relationships among family members who control the group. Similar reasons forced the Architect in the *Matrix* trilogy to come up with various versions.

Once the income tax authorities ripped off the veil of secrecy over portions of the Ambani matrix in the second half of the 1990s – as is evident from Alvi's papers – it had to be reconfigured anyway. Dhirubhai asked Mukesh to do so. Realizing that people like Anand Jain had the expertise to fix the problem, Mukesh sought their help. As each code had to be changed to hide the new reality, someone put an idea in Mukesh's head. What if the reconfiguration could be effected to his advantage? What if he could control the empire? What if he could build a new matrix that his younger brother, Anil, could never understand and, hence, could never break up the group?

As one of the sources close to Anil told me: 'The idea was never to steal Reliance from Anil and leave the younger brother in the lurch. The idea was never to wrest complete control. The idea was merely to protect Reliance's integrity and sanctity by making sure Anil couldn't effect a split. This was because Mukesh realized that, at some stage, Anil would ask for a break-up and his pound of flesh.' In retrospect, Mukesh was right.

How to do this? It was simple.

Since his father had given him the responsibility, Mukesh could choose his own team. And he got AJ to design the new matrix. So, only AJ would know the codes and understand the entire software. No one else would. The second step was to put Mukesh's men as directors in the various entities that formed parts of the system. Thus control over the hundreds of investment firms would be with Mukesh, via AJ. The third was not to let Anil get wind of it.

Years later, through trial and error, the matrix was as perfect as it could be. AJ was the Architect. Mukesh was the all-powerful Agent Smith. In their virtual world, the bug was Anil (or Neo) whose destiny had been written way back, even as AJ was rewriting the matrix. AJ knew that a tussle between Agent Smith and Neo was inevitable and destined. But Agent Smith had no idea about Neo's powers. And it took a long time for Neo to realize that he could destroy Agent Smith. But when Neo felt he had got rid of Agent Smith, the latter would reappear.

Now, let us take a look at the Reliance Matrix created by AJ. I can't tell you everything about it, but I can say that it was through this matrix that Mukesh exercised control over the Reliance empire. Anil had no idea that the overall family's control had shifted to just one member – his elder brother. As Morpheus tells Neo in the film, 'Unfortunately, no one can be told what the Matrix is. You have to see it for yourself.' If you want to believe Morpheus, he also said, 'The Matrix is everywhere, it's all around us, here even in this room. You can see it out your window, or on your television. You feel it when you go to work, or go to church or pay your taxes. It is the world that has been pulled over your eyes to blind you from the truth.' Although Morpheus is talking about the human world, the same is true about the investment matrix in the financial world.

Let's take the analogy further. In the movie, there's the seemingly real world, the one you see, touch, feel and understand through your senses. It is the world that's around you. The Reliance Matrix too has something that is in the public domain. Anyone can get details about it. Even Anil was aware of this aspect of the investment matrix.

RIL's website gave the shareholding pattern of the company. Indian promoters owned 12.63 per cent. Institutional investors (domestic and foreign) held 31.62 per cent, and 'others' (including the public, non-resident Indians and corporate bodies) had a 21.71 per cent stake. But there was something called 'persons acting in concert' which together owned a substantial 34.04 per cent.

It was these persons, acting in concert, who were critical. For they were really the hundreds of investment entities – the ones I have mentioned earlier – through which the Ambani family controlled, manageed and ran RIL. (Of course, after the split, Mukesh controls these firms, as he controls RIL. Anil's business will not be impacted by them.)

The RIL website also listed out fourteen firms – part of 'persons acting in concert' – which owned more than 1 per cent each in RIL. This was the part that you saw – the names of these firms, what they did, and who ran them. This was the 'seemingly-real' part of the Matrix. Anil knew about the existence of these fourteen firms. The names of some of these were quite esoteric – Sanchayita Mercantile, Tresta Trading,

Then came the spin. The two firms made a killing on the exchange because ONGC was listed at a higher price. Both sold a part of their holdings and earned profits, which went to Mukesh who, according to Anil's camp, owned the two companies. Ideally, RIL should have invested in the ONGC IPO as both are in similar businesses. RIL could have booked profits, instead of personally held firms. Here again was an extreme example of personal enrichment. Worse still, it was a case of acting against the interests of RIL and its shareholders. That's because the money to invest in the ONGC and TCS IPOs came from either RCIL or Reliance Infocomm. In both the Reliance-owned companies, it was RIL or the banks, which had provided the monies. So money was siphoned off from either RIL or the banks to invest in the two IPOs to create personal wealth.

The history of Smart Entrepreneur Solutions, now renamed as Synergy Entrepreneur Solutions, showed strong links with the Reliance group and Mukesh Ambani. Its original name was Reliance Communications Andaman & Nicobar. As mentioned earlier, in August 2003, it shifted its office to 806-807, Embassy Centre, Nariman Point, Mumbai. The last happened to be the headquarters of Jai Fibres, promoted by Anand Jain's family. Finally, its office was shifted to Dhirubhai Ambani Knowledge City, which is the centre of Reliance's telecom operations. Smart Entrepreneur Solutions had stakes in two companies, Jade Merchandise and Viddeshwar Leasing & Investment. The latter two had their offices in 84-A, Mittal Court, which, we know, was the hub of the investment firms owned and/or controlled by the Reliance group.

RIL issued a clarification about the two IPOs. It said that 'during the last few days, a well-orchestrated campaign has been unleashed about Reliance Industries Ltd, Reliance Infocomm Ltd and its chairman and managing director, Mukesh Ambani.

'The stories published in a section of the press today about the allotment of ONGC shares to two companies and the attempt to describe them as "two private unknown companies belonging to Reliance Industries Ltd chairman and managing director, Mukesh Ambani" are baseless and an exercise in misinterpretation and distortion of facts.

'Smart Entrepreneur Solutions Private Ltd and Smart Infosolutions Private Ltd, which applied for the IPO, are not unknown companies. Smart Entrepreneur Solutions employed over a thousand people and Smart Infosolutions around 3000 people. By no stretch of imagination can these be described as little or unknown.

'These companies do not belong to Mukesh Ambani.

'There is no mystery about the sources from which these companies obtained funds to subscribe to the public issue.

'These companies are owned by a Reliance Communications Infrastructure Ltd (RCIL) subsidiary. RCIL did not borrow from any banks or financial institutions to provide funds to two of its companies for subscribing to the IPO. In fact, RCIL provided funds from its own sources. It is libellous to say that the "money was diverted from Reliance Infocomm to these companies".

'It is also totally baseless to speculate that these companies "could have made a killing" on the day of the listing. In fact, over a crore of shares (of ONGC) are still held by these two companies, in spite of there being a significant volatility in the price of these shares.

'Reliance Industries Ltd will benefit from any gains that RCIL makes from these investments in the future.'

Finally, the Mukesh camp said that what was true of the ONGC IPO was also true of the investments in TCS. There was no private gain for Mukesh Ambani. There was no loss to RIL or its shareholders. In fact, both would benefit from these investments.

That should have been the end of this episode in the Ambani soap opera. All promoters use several entities to invest in shares. In fact, Anil's aide, Amitabh, was part of the investment matrix that regularly traded in equities and securities. And it's normal for corporates to use fronts to do that, instead of applying directly. But some of the dirt stuck to Mukesh. The rumour-mongers went to town with the following logic. Even if it was RCIL that provided money to buy ONGC and TCS shares, it would have indirectly come from RIL, which had virtually financed the telecom venture. If it was indeed RIL's money, it should have earned the entire profits, rather than get a 45 per cent share of it based on its 45 per cent stake in RCIL. But we'll have to see how the profits are apportioned to RIL since the 'Smart' firms sold their entire stake in ONGC in the open market a few months after this controversy.

Even as the Mukesh camp was breathing a sigh of relief that the 'Smart' controversy was over, yet another bomb was about to explode in Mukesh's face. Three days after the Mukesh camp released the 'not-so-smart' clarification, Anil's advisors revealed astonishing off-the-books accounting by Reliance Infocomm. It was not unlike what the US corporation, Enron, had done and which had sunk the energy major.

Enron had guts, ambition and the nerve to take unusual risks. It was at the cutting edge of how to take advantage of dramatic transformation in the global energy arena. For years, it enamoured jealous competitors, institutional investors and experts with its consistent fast-track growth. It just happened to be at the right place at the right time. It had the capability of taking advantage of any change. Whether it was the opening up of the power sector in India, the deregulation of retail power in the US, or the introduction of a new fuel, liquified natural gas, Enron was the leader.

Over time, people realized that one of the reasons for its amazing financial and market track record was the way it hid its losses. High-flying Enron managers took high risks that were bound to result in huge losses. But the company knew how to conceal them and keep them off its accounting books. It was simple: just transfer them off its books to little-known entities. The money needed for the transactions by these off-the-books entities would also come from Enron, either directly or indirectly. At one stage, $27 billion of Enron's $60 billion assets was parked in such firms. The bubble had to burst; in fact it was waiting for a tiny prick, which came in the form of a whistle-blower. It brought Enron down like a pack of cards and no one escaped unhurt from the debris.

According to a report (published in July 2002) by the Permanent Subcommittee on Investigations of the Committee on Governmental Affairs, United States Senate, 'Enron's multi-billion dollar, off-the-books activity was disclosed to the

Enron Board and received Board approval as an explicit strategy to improve Enron's financial statement. In fact, Enron's massive off-the-books activity could not have taken place without Board action to establish new special purpose entities, issue preferred Enron shares, and pledge Enron stock as the collateral for the deals to go forward. In the end, the Board knowingly allowed Enron to move at least $27 billion or almost 50 per cent of its assets off the balance sheet.

'During their interviews, only one Board member expressed concern about the percentage of Enron assets that no longer appeared on the company balance sheet; the remaining Board members expressed little or no concern. At the May 7 hearings, the three accounting and corporate governance experts testified that they were unaware of any other public company with such a high percentage of its assets off the balance sheet. Mr Sutton, former SEC chief accountant, said his "experience is that Enron is at the top of the scale in terms of the extent" of its off-the-books activity. Mr Campbell, who has extensive corporate and Board experience, testified that he "had never seen that amount, proportion of company's assets on off-balance sheet. Sometimes, it is appropriate to have assets off-balance sheet... but never to that extent."'

Reliance Infocomm did something similar. It too was forced to park huge losses in an unknown – known, if Mukesh's camp is to be believed – entity, Smart Entrepreneur Solutions.

Infocomm's was a high-growth, ambitious and slightly risky strategy. The aim was to rope in a huge number of customers who would put in money upfront. That way

Infocomm could recover a substantial chunk of its investments right from Day One. Ten million customers paying thousands of rupees each in advance would result in an income of several thousand crore rupees. A great business idea, but it flopped. As usual, customers were wary, as there were too many details in the fine print. Customers were also dissatisfied with the dealers who were marketing the Reliance services. Then came the Monsoon Hungama scheme, which did result in a multiple growth of Reliance telecom subscribers. This too had a catch. Many customers didn't pay up, resulting in bad debts or non-receivables of nearly Rs 3500 crore. Reliance Infocomm had assumed that only a fifth of its revenues would remain unpaid and, based on its revenues target, had kept aside Rs 470 crore for this purpose. But when the non-receivables ballooned to such a large extent, it created a problem.

That, too, for RIL.

During 2003-04, RIL entered into an agreement with Reliance Infocomm. The deal was that RIL would buy and sell mobile handsets to Infocomm's subscribers, maintain accounts, bill subscribers and collect the money due to Infocomm from its subscribers. One logic for doing this was that RIL would earn additional revenues if Infocomm could rope in the millions of customers it was targetting. Till the time Infocomm reached break-even levels and started earning profits, RIL would bear the financial burden of the telecom venture. No one thought what would happen in case things went wrong. And they did.

A large number of customers didn't pay, and the bad debt came on RIL's balance sheet. Its profit and loss account would have to provide for the losses of Rs 3500 crore. RIL, being a publicly listed company, wouldn't want to do that.

As usual, now the story got a bit murky.

Anil's camp said it was the younger brother who refused to sign RIL's financial accounts as long as Infocomm's losses were reflected in it. He wanted them out. So the agreement between RIL and Reliance Infocomm was terminated, Smart Entrepreneur Solutions agreed to buy Infocomm's bad debts and take it on its balance sheet. RCIL, which is Infocomm's parent company, provided the money to Smart Entrepreneur Solutions to pay RIL, the Ambani flagship managed to boost its profits, and everyone went back home in a happy state of mind.

That is, until the feud erupted. In another of his notes, Anil's advisor Amitabh alleged that parking of the bad debts in a privately owned firm amounted to 'wilful financial fraud, improper and misleading disclosure, and concealment of material information. The consequences of the above are criminal prosecution of all directors of Reliance Infocomm, namely Mr Mukesh Ambani, Mr Manoj Modi, Mr Anand Jain and Mr Bharat Goenka, apart from other civil and monetary liabilities.' There is legal ambiguity on whether this could be true. Legally, RCIL, Reliance Infocomm and Smart Entrepreneur Solutions are privately held companies and, therefore, no shareholders' interests were involved. On the flip side, since RIL (a publicly listed firm) had huge stakes in RCIL and Reliance Infocomm, one expected greater transparency within the Reliance group.

Mukesh's aides laughed at the proposition. First, they said that Anil never opposed the inclusion of Infocomm's non-receivables on RIL's balance sheet. They then added that if he did, as he claimed, then he practically forced RCIL and Reliance Infocomm to shift the bad debts from the books of a publicly listed company to a privately held one. If the losses had been transferred to Reliance Infocomm or RCIL, they would still have remained hidden, as both existed in the private domain and have no public shareholders. So it was Anil – if he had indeed opposed the move to include Infocomm's non-receivables on RIL's balance sheet – who made sure that the arrangement between RIL and Infocomm was terminated. Without it, the non-receivables couldn't be transferred to another firm.

There was nothing wrong about one company selling the bad debts to another. It is a routine commercial practice. Many firms do it regularly. As long as they are not subsidiaries of listed companies, there are no problems. (A subsidiary is a firm where the parent has a majority stake. In case of RCIL, RIL then owned 45 per cent stake.) More important in this case, RIL, the group's flagship that has lakhs of shareholders, got its money back as Smart Entrepreneur Solutions paid the entire amount to it while taking on the non-receivables debt on its balance sheet. That was good for RIL, its management and its investors. Finally, RIL's sale of non-receivables to Smart Entrepreneur Solutions was a move towards making the accounts more transparent. For it separated the accounts of the telecom group from RIL, which was essentially into exploration, refining and making petrochemicals.

However, as details came out in rapid succession, Mukesh & Co found it extremely difficult to detach controversy from Reliance Infocomm. The latter's network –

Rs 20,000 crore had been spent on it – failed to deliver positive signals to the public.

Initially, Anil had problems with Mukesh's 'sweat equity' in Infocomm, which the company wanted to give him at the face value of Re 1 per share. Later, it was disclosed that Mukesh's advisor, Manoj Modi, got 3 crore shares at the same price. The stake, given to the Modi-owned Kaizen Commercial, constituted 0.72 per cent of Infocomm's equity base of Rs 416.35 crore. (The percentage would have been higher at the time of allotment as Infocomm's capital was just over Rs 300 crore.)

But there was more. Three unknown Delhi-based firms – Prerna Auto, Softnet Traders and Consultants and Fairever Traders and Consultants – together received 1 crore shares (or 0.24 per cent) of Reliance Infocomm on 16 September 2002. That too at a price of Re 1 per share. As Anil's side claimed: 'These 1 crore shares were all given away, on a single day... just two months after the passing away of Dhirubhai Ambani, and just two months before the formal launch of Reliance Infocomm's business on 28 December 2002.'

No one knew anything about these three firms. Prerna Auto was owned by Lalit Goyal and Sapna Goyal; Fairever Traders by Anand Sharma and Anita Sharma; and Softnet Traders by Amit Gupta and Kamini Gupta. Their offices were in the same part of north Delhi – Ashok Vihar, Azadpur and Bungalow Road. And none of these existed. One day, Tony passed me a few photographs and said: 'I personally went to check if these offices really existed and clicked these photographs. You can see for yourself that these are shell companies.' One of the TV channels did the same exercise and came to the same conclusion.

Yet again, Anil decided to follow one of Sun Tzu's nuggets of war wisdom: 'Opportunities multiply as they are seized.' He launched fresh accusations at brother Mukesh. 'RIL paid a price of up to Rs 250 per share for its investments in Reliance Infocomm group companies, while Manoj Modi and these three new beneficiaries, who have now surfaced, have all paid only Re 1 per share – as usual, one more example of losses caused to RIL shareholders, for personal gains to others.'

What Anil was referring to was the fact that in one transaction relating to RCIL, Infocomm's parent company, RIL got 9 crore shares for Rs 2250 crore, or a price of Rs 250 per share. In fact, the average price that RIL paid for its entire 90 crore shares in RCIL was Rs 26 per share. But here were some unknown entities and Mukesh's friends who had got away with a ridiculously low price of Re 1 per share for Reliance Infocomm which, according to him, contributed the bulk of revenues earned by RCIL. More importantly, Modi & Co had earned huge paper profits – between 70 and 120 times the original investments – depending on varying valuations of Rs 30,000-50,000 crore made by four foreign research houses for Reliance's telecom business.

This was unacceptable to Anil. This was unfair to RIL. This was daylight robbery as far as the younger brother was concerned.

AJ found the charges unpalatable. 'RIL paid Re 1 per share for its direct holding (anything between 7 and 9 per cent) in Reliance Infocomm, which is the same as Manoj Modi and the three Delhi-based firms. It only paid a higher price for RCIL shares – and that too an average of Rs 26 per share – but the parent includes a number of other telecom-related operations. So, RCIL was valued higher than Infocomm.'

What the Mukesh camp would also like us to believe was that people like Lalit Goyal, Anand Sharma, Amit Gupta and Manoj Modi, as well as RIL, got the Infocomm shares at face value before the company commenced its operations. 'In such a scenario, there's a risk attached to business and shares are normally issued at face value. In other countries, promoters and their associates get shares for free. In India, because the law doesn't permit it, we issued them at face value. What's wrong with Manoj Modi getting the shares? Don't CEOs across the world get shares in their respective companies at discounted prices or for free?' questioned AJ.

While the two sides were debating valuations, paper profits, issue prices and corporate fairness, a political sub-plot was threatening to engulf the Reliance group.

A number of journalists were told that the owners of the three Delhi-based entities were linked to key politicians in the BJP; actually, just one of them was. Anil – who had perfected the science of target practice and who, every week, had selected a new target and trained his corporate guns on it – was now threatening to train his weapon on high-profile politicians. In a way, the younger brother was about to expose the 'unholy' nexus between corporates and those not-so-popular men in white khadis.

I was told – through the usual sources – that Lalit Goyal was related to Sudhanshu Mittal, who headed the BJP's election campaign in the recent Jharkhand state polls. Since

Sudhanshu is a key confidante of Pramod Mahajan, a senior BJP leader and former telecom minister, the circumstantial needle of suspicion pointed directly at Mahajan. The Mumbai-based BJP leader was clearly caught in the eye of the swirling Ambani storm.

When I called Sudhanshu to get his reaction, he went into a virtual monologue. 'It's easy to destroy any politician's image today, because baseless allegations seem to stick on us. Where's the scandal in this transaction (relating to Goyal's stake in Infocomm)? Goyal got the shares at the same price (Re 1 per share) as other shareholders of Reliance Infocomm. There was no favour. So, how can there be a scandal? When the shares were allotted, the company had not started its operations. There was also a question mark over the future of its CDMA technology. Why would anyone have paid a premium for such a company at that time?'

I had a nagging suspicion that Sudhanshu had probably talked to AJ. For they gave the same defence. Of course, I had no evidence for this observation. But Sudhanshu went on: 'The price paid is based on the situation at that particular moment. Now Merrill Lynch may say the company is valued at Rs 50,000 crore, but what's the credibility of such figures? During the height of the dot-com boom, my company was valued at Rs 5000 crore. When I closed it, it had incurred a loss of Rs 3.50 crore and there were no takers for it.

'Goyal is a businessman in his own right and hasn't got shares because of his proximity to me. He earns an annual salary of Rs 2.5 crore and I would like to trade places with him any day, instead of being in politics. He has a successful business empire worth Rs 600 crore and was a promoter of the

Lifespring chain and probably the first to introduce laminated tiles in India. He has interests in infrastructure and stays in one of the best penthouses in Gurgaon (Delhi's upcoming and fast-growing satellite city).

'All these allegations are to malign my image. I have a lot of enemies in political circles who'd love to see me in this situation. Imagine, one TV channel used a secret camera to trace me in my office and to find out if I have links with Goyal. Am I a criminal or a man on the run? Am I an American fugitive or something? It's ridiculous. Remember that no new company can demand a premium during the initial share allotment unless it has commenced operations. Bharti (the cellular operator) did get a premium during its IPO. But it had one million subscribers at that time. Now if RIL paid a much higher price for RCIL, that's a problem with the decisions taken by the Reliance management and has got nothing to do with me or Goyal.'

Pramod Mahajan also got into the act to clear his name. He gave an interview to *India Today*, on his 'connections with the House of Ambanis'. He felt, like Sudhanshu, that the media was deliberately maligning his name. But none of the newspapers or magazines had been able to prove conclusively that he had taken decisions that helped Reliance during his tenure as the telecom minister. 'I want to know what decision of mine has helped RIL or Reliance Infocomm? Yes, I took the decision to issue a stamp in the memory of Dhirubhai Ambani after his death. If it's a crime then I am ready to pay a price for it.' He further clarified that it was indeed the NDA coalition, led by the BJP, that permitted the introduction of the wireless-in-local-loop (WLL) technology, which is used by Reliance

Infocomm. 'But the decision was taken by Ram Vilas Paswan a full year before I became the communications minister.' Yes, it is true that Mahajan fully endorsed the migration to a uniform licence regime which, according to Infocomm's competitors, would end up helping Infocomm to a large extent. '... but the decision (on uniform licence regime) was taken by Arun Shourie,' who became the telecom minister after Mahajan was eased out in a Cabinet reshuffle. Still, Mahajan's name kept getting dragged in the Reliance imbroglio at regular intervals. The reason: there were just too many uncanny coincidences in several of Infocomm's investment dealings that pointed a finger in the politician's direction.

It was the *Asian Age* that unravelled most of these links. It was this newspaper that was at the forefront of a campaign against Mahajan. For weeks, it kept needling him with almost daily front-page fliers that frantically tried to connect Mahajan's son, Rahul, his daughter, Poonam, and his son-in-law, Anand Rao, with Reliance Infocomm. Most of these, however, seemed contrived.

But some of the articles were worth a second look.

First, *Asian Age* found a link between the three Delhi-based firms – Prerna Auto, Fairever Traders and Softnet Traders – all of which subsequently shifted their offices to Mumbai. One of the Mumbai-based firms, Unnati Mercantile, which was part owner of the three entities, had both Lalit Goyal (of Prerna Auto) and Anand Sharma (of Fairever Traders) as directors. Clearly, the two knew each other. Later, it was revealed that Fairever Traders' Mumbai address was the same as that of Global E-Serve. Both were housed in Shriram Mills, Lower Parel, Mumbai. This meant that there was a connection between Fairever Traders and Global E-Serve.

One of the owner/directors of Global E-Serve was Ashish Deora, who admitted to his connections with Fairever Traders. Ashish was also a director/owner in India Online Network, which later changed its name to IOL Broadband. Another director/owner of IOL Broadband is V. Ramanand Rao, popularly known as Anand Rao, who is Pramod Mahajan's son-in-law. Here was another association between Mahajan and Infocomm. *Indian Express* called it 'the politics of association'. The newspaper said it was 'association' because despite the lack of a clear-cut paper trail, there was enough 'to kickstart a political slugfest'.

The Mukesh camp provided the final twist. In a public statement, it admitted that the 1 crore shares given to Prerna Auto, Fairever Traders and Softnet Traders were meant for Deora. It was Deora who had insisted that the shares be issued to the three companies.

It was a classic case of distancing the real owner from the transaction. Infocomm gave the stake to Delhi-based entities, whose directors were not directly connected to the real beneficiary. These companies moved their offices to Mumbai. But they were actually controlled by someone else. In this case, it seemed to be Ashish Deora.

Or was it someone else?

But why was Deora given the shares in the first place? Infocomm's press release said the shares given to Deora were from 'shares that were transferred to a trust, intended for the benefit of employees and business associates. These were to be used for the purpose for which they have been allotted. The trust is authorized to sell their shares to business associates of Reliance.' How was Deora a business associate? 'Since Mr Ashish Deora had prior expertise and experience in obtaining in-building permissions, his services were retained by RIC (Reliance Infocomm) as part of their fibre-optic/broadband project in Greater Mumbai.

'RIC agreed to compensate Mr Ashish Deora by way of a nominal compensation per building upfront and the remaining via appreciation on equity shares of RIC to be sold to him or his nominees by the Trust. Using this methodology, RIC was able to link compensation to performance... Pursuant to this understanding, the Trust sold equity shares to three nominee companies controlled by Mr Ashish Deora.'

Now comes the moot question: was Deora the key beneficiary, or was it IOL Broadband? IOL Broadband had the all-round expertise that Infocomm required. According to an article on a website (www.networkmagazineindia.com), IOL Broadband 'has already installed an end-to-end optical fibre network in Mumbai. IOL launched its SpeedMelon broadband Internet service in June 2001... IOL began work on its DWDM fibre optic network about a year back when it started laying the backbone, a 48-core fibre optic cable with a capacity of 48 Gbps. The 100 km backbone runs through Mumbai city, beginning at Cuffe Parade in south Mumbai and extending northwards to Andheri.'

The question was: Why did Infocomm choose only Ashish Deora, and not IOL Broadband, for its services? There were no answers.

All we know is that Infocomm denied any connections with Mahajan. The BJP leader denied it too. In the interview to *India Today*, he said: 'I solemnly affirm that my wife Rekha, my son Rahul, my daughter Poonam and my son-in-law Anand Rao have not got any shares (of Infocomm) or pecuniary benefit. If someone wants to insinuate that my friends' shares are mine then by this logic any politician can be accused of wrongdoing. Rahul is not... a promoter of India Online (which later became IOL Broadband). Nor is Poonam. Yes, my son-in-law is in the company but he has been there even before his engagement to my daughter.'

Even Deora sang the same tune. In an interview with *Indian Express*, he said: 'It is quite unfair to drag former telecom minister Pramod Mahajan into the picture. He has nothing to do with my company's operations... When Rao and I set up the company, we had no political connections or ambitions... I'm caught in the crossfire between some big people.'

He was indeed, for Infocomm took back the 1 crore shares from Deora. According to the Infocomm release, Deora couldn't fulfil his obligations and, hence, the shares were returned to the Trust. 'The three companies or Mr Ashish Deora do not hold any shares of RIC (Reliance Infocomm). This should rest all attempts to distort the issue of allocation of shares to Mr Deora or his companies... This disinformation campaign focused in the beginning on allotment of shares with a view to spread the canard that the shares were allotted to certain companies and individuals at Re 1 per share while Reliance Industries Ltd, or RIL, had to pay many times more. This is totally false, as no shares to RIL have been issued at a premium till date.'

Try as they might, Mukesh's aides were unable to prevent the attacks on Infocomm. It seemed that Infocomm had become a public relations time bomb, ticking away to its final moment of destruction. Even politicians got into the act of attacking Infocomm.

One of these was Dayanidhi Maran, the DMK leader from Tamil Nadu, who became the telecom minister in the UPA government under controversial circumstances. In 2004, when he was given the portfolio, his critics screamed that there would be a conflict of interests between his post and his family's business interests. Dayanidhi's brother, Kalanidhi, ran profitable operations relating to Television-Cable-Content, and it was obvious that some of the decisions in the telecom sector would impact them. But Dayanidhi said there was no conflict as he was no longer a businessman. In addition, all decisions on cable network would be taken by the I&B ministry, and not his.

But controversy continued to dog him. It was inevitable. For Dayanidhi was one of the few politicians who decided to take on Reliance – head-on.

As part of its telecom strategy, Reliance expanded its operations, especially in the US. For a telecom operator, ISD (International Speed Dialling) contributes huge profits, and Reliance was keen to capture a sizeable share of the market. But there was a catch. To cut costs and boost profits, the Ambanis opted for an innovative way to route their international calls. As one of Mukesh's Delhi-based advisors told me: 'We invested in setting up the infrastructure. And used it to route calls originating from the US and land them at our own sites in India. Only then did we route them to specific destinations using the BSNL or other networks.'

In effect, what Reliance did was to show incoming

international calls as local ones; as calls originating from their Indian base. In effect, Reliance thus paid charges only for local/STD calls for using the networks of BSNL and others. Since the network usage rates for ISD calls are much higher, Reliance ended up making huge savings in costs. It was a brilliant idea.

The problem: as per existing laws it was illegal. Technically, Reliance might have been right. Legally, it was operating in a grey area. In fact, such re-routing was termed 'grey market calls'. Finally, BSNL caught on. So did DoT (Department of Telecommunications). The Telecom Regulatory Authority of India (TRAI) came in the line of fire. TRAI's consultation papers hinted that existing rules might lead to improper practices. 'A major point made in the context of the recent complaints regarding grey market traffic has been that the authority's ADC (access deficit charges) regime has resulted in a large arbitrage opportunity... In comparison to the ADC regime notified in January 2003, the revised ADC regime notified in October 2003 made the grey market situation worse...,' observed TRAI's amendments issued on 6 January 2005. It added: 'The issue of grey market international calls continues to be relevant, as is indicated by anecdotal evidence and complaints submitted to the Authority, and possibly also by the decline in the incoming international call minutes per subscriber.'

But TRAI did nothing to stop it. Pradip Baijal, the Authority's outspoken, suave and media-savvy chairman, said he couldn't. 'I knew it could happen but BSNL told me categorically that it can check the grey market traffic. I had no choice but to keep the ADC on international calls high and maintain the large difference between the ADC on international and national calls. I had to continue with the ADC regime on per-minute basis, rather than as a percentage of revenues. Both were to ensure the profitability of the (state-owned) BSNL and to subsidize it for its unviable operations (in rural areas). It may have been an error of judgment, but everything was placed in Parliament. It could have changed them, amended them, annulled them.'

When the telecom regulator got to know about the grey market, it transferred the case to DoT. 'This was what I had to do. The Act stated that any dispute between operators had to be resolved by DoT and the telecom appellate,' an agitated Baijal told me. Reliance Infocomm was asked to pay up the difference between the ADC charges, and a penalty of Rs 150 crore was imposed on the company. Infocomm paid up the difference, but legally opposed the penalty in the Supreme Court. What was important was that Dayanidhi was unwilling to give up the fight. He had vowed to punish the guilty. He had vowed to bring them down on their knees. He had decided to hit Reliance where it hurt the most – Mukesh's Infocomm.

Shankar Adwal was Reliance's point man to solve any telecom-related crisis for Reliance. Based in Delhi, Shankar knew the telecom ministry and DoT inside out, like the back of his hand. He was also one of those liaison persons who shied away from public glare, worked efficiently behind the scenes and believed in getting work done. He had to somehow stall the increasing legal, public and political pressure because of the illegal re-routing case.

But whatever he did, the results weren't showing. Not any more. Not since Dayanidhi had taken over as the telecom minister, and the two Ambani brothers had gone public with their bitter dispute to divide the Reliance spoils. His magic touch was failing – visibly. Over time, the desperate Shankar concluded the telecom case had gone out of hand because of the sibling rivalry. He told friends that if the two brothers had been together, the DoT wouldn't have gone this far. 'The fight has diminished the political clout of the Ambanis; now anyone, anywhere thinks he can go after Reliance,' he told one of his friends. In private moments, he felt that the DoT was deliberately targeting Reliance. That there were factors other than legal that were responsible for the present state of affairs. To somehow win the media campaign, his battery of loyalists went on the offensive. They leaked information that Infocomm was not the only company that was guilty of any wrongdoing. Almost all the telecom operators had committed irregularities. Documents relating to them were freely available. But, for the media and the public, the case against Reliance was more interesting.

To be fair to Shankar, he was dead against the re-routing strategy, but one powerful person around Mukesh cowed him down. When his friends asked him who that manager was, he smiled and answered: 'Someone very high up in the hierarchy. But it was not Mukesh Ambani.' I knew who that manager was, but I didn't have any proof against him. Only later did *The Times of India* reveal the 'smoking gun' evidence that international call re-routing was Manoj Modi's idea and it was he who had pushed it through despite opposition from senior Reliance managers.

Shankar's opposition to call re-routing was shared by none other than Akhil Gupta who, in early 2004 was CEO (corporate development) of Reliance Infocomm. Akhil's views were sensitive, critical and important. For, he was one of Mukesh's closest aides. One can gauge their friendship – and Akhil's proximity to the Ambani family – by the fact that he was the only outsider (non-family member) who had an apartment in Sea Wind. Akhil, a US citizen, stayed with the Ambanis at the latter's residence while he was in Mumbai during various business-related trips.

In March 2004, Akhil wrote an e-mail to Mukesh Ambani. 'I have reservations regarding the 12 cents per minute to all phones (scheme) and not just (Reliance phones). Within seven to ten days of our commercial launch, BSNL will know. It will clearly be established that we are violating in spirit if not the law and avoiding paying ADC (access deficit charge) to BSNL or (the) government. I will be surprised if TRAI/ other government agencies do not move to reverse this. If we have to reverse, how do we go back to consumers? We need to create a softer image of Reliance Infocomm in NRI's minds.' (It was basically this NRI scheme(s) where the illegal re-routing of international calls took place, and most of these calls originated from NRIs in the US, a market which was under Akhil's direct charge.) In the same e-mail, Akhil offered to opt out of overseeing the NRI scheme and also hinted who was the brain behind it. 'I suggest that we hand over the sponsorship (or management) of the NRI scheme to MM/BDK (Manoj Modi / B.D. Khurana)... I have three to four weeks before we go on vacation. I would assist the new sponsors during this time.'

Mukesh stepped in to correct the situation. The management – and responsibilities – of the Infocomm project was divided with Modi handling regulatory and legal issues in India and Akhil looking after marketing work in the US. After the government began investigating Infocomm's call re-routing strategy, Akhil shot off another e-mail to the Boss in December 2004. This time he made it clear that it was Modi who was responsible for Infocomm's legal mess. 'I have heard from several sources now that MM's (Manoj Modi) office is spreading rumours that (I) was responsible for deciding to modify caller line identification and not pay ADC. As you can see from my previous e-mail, I had opposed it and put my warning in writing... Would you please help in stopping this unethical nonsense from spreading and set the record straight... It is very painful to see us paying huge penalties, spoiling our name and the person responsible gets to blame someone else. What a shame!' A few weeks later, Akhil resigned from Infocomm.

Akhil's resignation itself was a surprise as he was so close to the Ambani family. Anil's aides started a whisper campaign. One of them told me: 'Akhil Gupta left because he couldn't stand Modi. He resigned because he had asked Mukesh to choose between him and Modi. Mukesh stood by Modi, and Akhil had no option but to leave. In the entire Ambani war, there are several sideshows — Tony (Anil's side) vs Shankar Adwal and Balu (an old-time lobbyist since Dhirubhai's days) in Delhi, Amitabh Jhunjhunwala vs Anand Jain in Mumbai, and Akhil vs Modi.' (Whatever the truth, Akhil joined the US-based fund manager, Blackstone, which plans to invest nearly $2 billion in the Indian capital markets.)

But one question still remained unanswered: who had leaked Akhil's e-mails? Was it the Anil side, which had stumbled upon them? Was it Akhil himself since he was in Delhi and Mumbai, while travelling with Blackstone's CEO, when the e-mails were leaked on 18 May 2005? Or was it someone in DoT, telecom ministry or the Central Bureau of Investigation (CBI) since all three had access to Reliance Infocomm's documents and records?

Mukesh's side blamed Anil, who said it was Akhil who gave the e-mails to journalists. Tony's spin was even better: 'After Akhil joined Blackstone, he got scared that if his name was involved in the Infocomm imbroglio, he might be investigated by the US-based market regulator, the Securities and Exchange Commission. So, during his India trip, he met a few journalists from *The Times of India*, *Hindustan Times* and one more publication. But only TOI carried his e-mails.'

But the Akhil episode didn't end there.

Three days later, *Asian Age* got hold of more damaging documents. More e-mails from Modi, in response to Akhil's reservations on the NRI scheme. When Mukesh asked Modi to clarify, the latter initially wrote that 'the regulator (TRAI) could raise certain issues of re-routing of calls and changing of caller ID. However, we are very confident that we will be able to handle the same using our good offices in the government and other agencies. I assure you there is no cause for concern, please allow us to go ahead with our project. The risk-to-benefit ratio is very high.' However, some time later, Modi was more confident about his scheme. In his second e-mail, he was sure there would be no problems with the regulator. 'With reference to my e-mail sent last week clarifying concerns raised by Mr Akhil Gupta I want to inform you that I have personally spoken to the regulator PB (Pradip Baijal, chairman, TRAI) today and have convinced him of our intention. We are also ensuring that he's taken good care of. Respectfully, MM.'

Infocomm managers refused to comment on the veracity of this e-mail. In fact, they said 'no comments' as the telecom case was still pending in the Supreme Court. But Baijal decided to take the bull by the horn. In an exclusive telephonic interview to *Outlook*, he said: 'The e-mail seems to be a fraud. I am consulting my lawyers to take action against the publications which printed it. I have not met Manoj Modi for a year. Before that, I met him during presentations that Reliance Infocomm gave during the height of the CDMA-GSM controversy (Reliance, which had CDMA technology, was accused by the GSM operators of offering services that violated the clauses included in Reliance's telecom licences). Modi was one of the Reliance managers who was present at the meetings. We've never discussed the re-routing issue. If I was supporting Reliance on it, why would I have forwarded the complaint I received to the vigilance wing of the DoT? Couldn't I have just sat on it without taking any action? And, even if you think that I favoured Reliance, do you think Modi is the kind of person who would put down such sensitive things in an e-mail? Wouldn't he have just walked into the boss' room and discussed it verbally with him?' However, Modi wasn't available for any comments.

(The *Asian Age* leak provided a few hints that probably it wasn't Akhil who was leaking these e-mails. Logically, Akhil would have access to Modi's replies, as Mukesh may have forwarded them to him. But the set of e-mails were given to two journalists – in TOI and *Asian Age* – both of whom were extremely close to Anil. In fact, since the beginning of the public feud, both had been fed documents and information from the Anil camp. Both had completely sided with Anil. I had a thought: could it be that Akhil had passed on these e-mails to Anil, who timed the leaks to coincide with Akhil's India visit to create confusion?)

Suddenly, there were too many cats out of the bag. Shankar had opposed the scheme. So had Mukesh's key business strategist and friend, Akhil. But Modi had bulldozed his way through. More important, the telecom regulator was probably aware of the scheme. TRAI's Baijal seemed to have given his green signal. Reliance Infocomm was still fighting the case in the Supreme Court and didn't seem to be gaining lost ground. It seemed it had an impossible task ahead, especially with the revelations that many important people knew about the possible irregularities.

It was one of Anil's aides who told me how this could have been nipped in the bud and how Infocomm had botched up the telecom case. 'Infocomm should have paid the charges and the penalty, instead of fighting the might of the government. That's what the late Dhirubhai did. It was his policy to pay up in case there was a dispute, or in case the issue threatened to become a nightmare. But, for some reason, Mukesh decided to fight back, and take on the telecom ministry. That was a blunder.' Another of Mukesh's blunders was that he was too emotional about Infocomm. In the process, he focused all his attention on Infocomm, used RIL cashflows to finance the telecom venture, and somehow gave the impression that he wasn't interested in using RIL finances to help the projects that were being planned by his younger brother. For Anil, who was striving hard to establish himself as a builder of mega projects – like his elder brother – this seemed unfair and unjustified. That was why, early on in his battle, Anil decided to permanently dent Infocomm's credibility.

5
Riding the RIL Tiger

> *The good fighters of old first put themselves beyond the possibility of defeat, and then waited for an opportunity of defeating the enemy.*
>
> — The Art of War by Sun Tzu

> *Make your brother so impotent that he cannot retaliate; make him so inconsequential that he cannot fight back.*
>
> — Ambani interpretation

Mukesh and Anil had not spoken to each other for years. Probably not since their father died in July 2002. Certainly not since November 2002, when secret, back-room negotiations began between the two camps to discuss the modalities of how to split the Reliance group.

It was funny to watch the two brothers talk to each other through the media during their public tussle. Anil would tell journalists that he was willing to talk to Mukesh, but without the presence of his advisors like Anand Jain. Mukesh would leak letters to TV channels saying he too was keen to talk to Anil. But they would actually communicate through letters and e-mails, which were repeatedly leaked to the media. When it came to issues like dividing the Reliance spoils, it was the advisors who would sit at the negotiating table. Therefore, it became big news when the two brothers met at a public gathering for the first time since their public bickering began. The occasion was *The Economic Times* annual awards ceremony on 27 November 2004. Here I will allow *The Economic Times* to hog the limelight because its correspondent was right there at the spot where it all happened.

'At the star-studded night of *The Economic Times* Awards for Corporate Excellence on Saturday in Mumbai, Mukesh and Anil Ambani smiled, then firmly shook hands. The smile may have been a bit tentative, especially Anil's to Mukesh, but the vice-like grip of the two powerful hands seemed to suggest that even though all may not be well at the Ambani household, all is not lost either. Miss World and Bollywood supersiren Priyanka Chopra, sitting a few seats away from Anil Ambani, gaped with her mouth open. She could well have been saying, "Oh brother!"

'Mukesh Ambani was the first to arrive at the venue – Hilton Towers in Nariman Point – with Anand Jain and cousins, the Meswani brothers, in tow a good ten minutes before the ceremony. The medium-built Ambani walked tall, straight down the aisle, but carefully avoiding the media glare, and took his seat on row one (to the right of the stage)... Younger brother, the dapper Anil Ambani, walked in just in time for the function with woman-in-red, his gorgeous wife Tina. Instead of walking down the middle like his brother did, he chose to remain on the sidelines – all eyes on him and his eyes on none – and while he did grace row one also, he insisted on sitting in the other corner... And then, you could hear a pin drop. Just a few minutes before the curtains were about to go down on corporate India's biggest spectacle, Ambani Sr got up and crossed over to the other side, briskly shaking hands with arch-rival and GSM czar Sunil Mittal, before walking all the way to the end and extending a warm handshake to Anil's wife Tina. "Hi Muks," said the one-time queen of Bollywood to Big Brother-in-Law Mukesh.

'And then, the moment corporate India was waiting for. Will he, won't he? For that brief flash, all eyes were riveted to that one corner of Hilton Poolside lawns where the two brothers were within kissing distance of each other – "Hi Anil," Mukesh broke the ice, putting his hand out, the clasp of the shake firm and reassuring. "Hi Boss," acknowledged Anil, without leaving his chair, but looking straight into his brother's eye.'

But that turned out to be a one-off event. The handshake didn't result in any more talks between the two, except for pleasantries exchanged in public. The advisors from both sides – many of whom were also involved in trying to bring the brothers together or help them reach an amicable agreement – got totally frustrated with the lack of communication between Mukesh and Anil. In time, they began to joke about their miseries and failures.

'Why don't they talk? Why do they just write letters saying they want to talk? Who's stopping them? Do they know they are doing what B-Schools will never teach? And both of them have been to American business schools! Sometimes, I feel like shaking my boss and forcing him to sit at the table with his brother. After all, they live in the same building (Sea Wind). Even if they don't want to go to each other's apartment, can't they meet on the stairs or the front lawns or something,' one of them told me in a mocking and sarcastic tone.

The same advisor added: 'Alam, do you think we should allow these two brothers to run such large businesses? Do you think the Reliance shareholders can feel safe with two brothers, who can't even talk to each other? Don't you feel someone else should manage the group.' He was obviously not serious, but the message was clear. How can Mukesh and Anil be expected to take critical decisions about their companies, when they have such bloated egos that they can't even sit at the negotiating table and patiently discuss ways to split the group amongst them?

Another aide kept complaining about his holidays, or the lack of them. Each time I would speak to him, he would start by saying how he hadn't been able to take leave because of the feuding Ambanis. 'I had to cancel my New Year's trip. Now, I can't even plan one until this gets over. Worse, the two Ambanis aren't even talking.' A few weeks later, he told me he was definitely going to take a break in June 2005. 'I don't care whether the two brothers patch up or split. I'm going.'

His cribbings continued, as did the sibling rivalry. It was a soap opera with no ending. Or so it seemed in May 2005. But, at the end of the day, the Ambani war was about the flagship, the cash-cow parent company RIL. While Anil was sniping away at Reliance Infocomm and the secrecy behind the family's holdings, he was worried about his place, stature and role in RIL. He was scared that he might be thrown out of RIL and be left with nothing. He was terrified that he would be on the road – literally – with nothing to show for himself, apart from the Ambani name.

For months, I had heard the rumour that Nita, Mukesh's wife, was likely to be inducted on RIL's board. But there was no way I could write about it; there was not even a shred of evidence. But the 'Nita' factor and her growing influence in Reliance's businesses continued to bother Anil and his advisors. They were sure Nita's ambition was to play an increasingly bigger role in Reliance affairs; that the pinnacle of her craving would be a RIL directorship. True or not – the Mukesh camp denied it categorically – it further distanced Anil from Mukesh.

Anil thought the brain behind Nita's proposed induction – and behind attempts to exclude him from RIL – was none other than AJ. He had heard from several friends that AJ had openly talked about how they (Mukesh's camp) could get rid of Anil in no time. In early 2005, Anil wrote a letter to RIL's board members accusing AJ of hatching a plot to throw him out of RIL. He informed the board of an incident 'which reflects the premeditated idea generated by Anand Jain... Jain, who holds no official position in RIL, called up Uday Kotak, a prominent banker, and said to him: "Why doesn't Anil understand... we have more than 50 per cent voting power... we can call an extraordinary general meeting (EGM), and throw him out of RIL any time we like."'

Tony told me of another incident involving AJ. 'A journalist called up Anand Jain and put the conversation on speakerphone. I can vouch for it.' Anil had written a letter urging the RIL board to hold an early meeting to discuss issues that had become public – or rather, had been leaked to the media by Anil's camp. This journalist wanted AJ to respond to it. AJ replied: 'Koi bhi chaprasi chitthi likhega toh board meeting kar lenge kya (If any peon writes a letter, will we call a board meeting?)'

Such incidents, true or not, left Anil fuming. He was convinced that there was a deep-rooted conspiracy to throw him out of RIL. He knew that without a foothold in RIL's boardroom, he had no chance of bringing Mukesh to the table. He had no future without RIL.

27 July 2004. That day Anil became certain that he was being sidelined in RIL, and that it was a precursor to his final ejection from the company's board. That Tuesday, the RIL board met for one of its regular meetings, which was held at noon at Reliance Centre, Walchand Hirachand Marg, Ballard Estate, Mumbai. Ironically, this was the headquarters of Reliance Energy, which was managed by Anil Ambani. In a sense, the board meeting was held in Anil's own corporate backyard. As he saw it, it was an attempt to stab him in the back.

According to Anil, the meeting had the makings of a classic corporate coup.

The main agenda seemed harmless. The four listed items in the supplementary agenda that was circulated to all the directors didn't reveal much. One was to 'approve the appointment of Shri H.S. Kohli as Trustee and Chairman of the Board of Trustees of various Provident Fund Trusts of the Company.' Another was to 'approve making an investment of upto US $200,000 in the Share Capital of Reliance Brazil LLC and making it a subsidiary of the Company.' A third stated: 'To note the Minutes of the Finance Committee of Directors held on 26 July 2004.'

But there was one item that had the potential to destroy Anil. The younger brother couldn't have got any hint from its title which read: 'To approve constitution of a "Health, Safety and Environment" Committee and to confirm authorities hitherto delegated by the Board to Committees of Directors/Directors/Executives as also confirm such of those delegated authorities as are subsisting and to consider modifications, if any.' Its details were revealed at the last minute as Item No. 2 of the additional agenda. Even then, a cursory glance wouldn't have revealed anything. Annexure A attached with this item gave out details under the heading: 'particulars of authorities of executive directors, executives and committee of directors.' The landmines were hidden here.

'Shri Mukesh D. Ambani, as Chairman and Managing Director being accountable and responsible to the Board, will exercise the specific power to allocate, delegate or assign specific duties, responsibilities and powers to Managing Director(s), Whole-time Director(s) and all executives and employees and to vary or revoke all or any duties, responsibilities or powers so allocated, delegated or assigned to such persons…' Nothing seemed wrong or out of place at this juncture. Then it went on.

'As hitherto, the Vice Chairman and Managing Director will perform his duties as Vice Chairman and Managing Director with regard to all the work of the Company and Shri Anil D. Ambani as Vice Chairman and Managing Director will manage and superintend such business and carry out the orders and directions given by the Board from time to time in all respects and conform to and comply with all such directions and regulations as may from time to time be given and made by the Board and his functions will be under the overall authority of the Chairman and Managing Director.'

At the board meeting, the directors 'resolved that pursuant to all applicable provisions of the Companies Act of 1956 (the "Act") and Articles of Association of the Company (the "Articles")... The Board of Directors (the "Board"), hereby confirms and redefines the powers and authorities conferred on the Chairman and Managing Director, Vice Chairman and Managing Director, Whole-time Directors and Executives as under...' And it repeated the things that were mentioned in Annexure A of Item No. 2.

The changes in the power structure stunned Anil. As he pointed out later, he did not raise the issue at the board meeting as he did not want to do so in front of all the RIL directors. But he clearly saw it as an attempt to completely clip his wings. He would now have to report to Mukesh. They were not equals any more. This was Mukesh's way to show who the Boss was. Anil would not allow this to happen. Just because Mukesh was called the 'Boss' did not mean he could walk all over Anil. After all, Anil was part of the family. He was also Dhirubhai's son. He should have the same powers as Mukesh in RIL.

This was war. It started with an exchange of several letters and e-mails.

Anil to K. Sethuraman, RIL's secretarial staff, 28 July 2004, 11.51 a.m.: 'As discussed personally on the phone this morning,

1. Please send me the additional agenda items tabled on the board yesterday.
2. Please do not finalize the minutes of yesterday's board meeting especially on the additional agenda items without my express approval.

'I have mentioned to you several times that I am not supportive of having additional agenda items on the Board, unless and until they have my prior clearance. You have not followed this for yesterday's board meeting.

'Henceforth, as a policy, please ensure that no additional agenda items are tabled unless they are of emergency nature (none of the items tabled yesterday were urgent enough and could have been duly thought over and put as items in the main agenda).'

Anil to Sethuraman, 29 July 2004, 04.16 p.m.: '… Additional agenda items are not to be tabled at RIL Board meetings, unless and until I have been shown the relevant papers, and have given my prior approval. The minutes of meetings of any RIL Board Committees on which I am a member are not to be finalized without my consent, either written, or through my actual presence, at such meetings. I must receive prior intimation/advance notice of all committee meetings and either you will receive my written consent or telephonic consent or my decision to personally attend.

'KS, I must put on record that I am surprised and concerned that substantive matters of the nature covered under additional agenda item No. 2 have been surreptitiously sought to be taken by you through the RIL Board Meeting in the above manner, without any prior briefing or discussion with me. So much so that after the Board Meeting you abstracted the additional agenda item papers, and I had to again call you personally for the papers, as also asked vide my enclosed e-mail yesterday.

'I also find it strange that when I called you this morning and enquired about the origin of the additional agenda item No. 2, and who had drafted the same, you were first not willing to give me any information, and when I persisted, you said the papers were given to you by MDA (Mukesh D. Ambani)/sent by MDA. I am surprised that you deemed it fit not to bring all this to my notice, as you would obviously have received the papers well in advance.

'It further surprises me that you have not conducted your own due diligence, and/or had the courtesy, of discussing these agenda items with me, or even informing me of the same, as to what were the previous resolutions, the proposed modifications, and the impact thereof. So much for professionalism and ethics!

'In the future, if you have any reservations about meeting me, or discussing such matters (for reasons best known only to yourself), please depute SP (Surendra Pipara) or any other person from your team with the relevant papers, to brief me and keep me fully informed, and to ascertain my views before taking any further steps.'

Minutes later, Anil flashed off an e-mail to his elder brother.

Anil to Mukesh, 29 July 2004, 04.32 p.m.: 'I wish to bring to your attention the following issues, which I consciously did not raise at the RIL Board Meeting on 27.7.2004, so as to avoid embarrassment of any kind to anyone, in the presence of other Board members and our senior management team. This e-mail would have been totally unnecessary, if the relevant papers had been sent in advance, as we could have then pre-discussed and agreed (sic) the necessary resolution for the Board.

'The additional agenda item No. 2 dealing, inter alia, with confirmation of the authorities delegated by the Board ... was tabled without my knowledge and/or consent. The contents of Annexure A to the additional agenda item No. 2 are at variation with the existing delegation of powers to the Managing Directors, as per record.

'There has been no discussion between us, and/or other Directors, either before the Board meeting on 27.7.2004, or at the said Board meeting, about the proposed modifications, if any, that should be considered to the existing delegation of powers to the Managing Directors of RIL (the only discussion at the Board meeting on this additional agenda item was in regard to the constitution of the Health, Safety and Environment Committee). Accordingly, there is no question of additional agenda item no. 2 being approved by the Board.

'Till you and I have discussed and agreed (sic) this matter, I have informed KS and SP, as per my e-mail of 28.7.2004... not to finalize the minutes of the RIL Board meeting on 27.7.2004, especially on the additional agenda item No. 2, without my approval... KS informed me that additional agenda item No. 2 as above was tabled on instructions from your office and, hence, I am sending this e-mail to you, to ensure that there is no misunderstanding or miscommunication, and we discuss and mutually agree upon the forward path on this and other future issues, so that our energies are used productively and constructively.

'I request you to treat the above mail in the spirit of dialogue in which it is sent.'

Despite the e-mails, Anil received the draft minutes of the July board meeting, including the board's consent on additional agenda item No. 2. As expected, Anil went berserk.

Anil to Vinod Ambani, RIL's company secretary, whose office had delivered the draft minutes, 29 July 2004, 07.58 p.m.: 'My office tried to get in touch with you, but you were unavailable. I was informed that you are out of town. At the outset, I am surprised to receive draft minutes of the Board Meeting of 27 July, from you, as in the last many years, all RIL Board matters have been handled by K. Sethuraman and Surendra Pipara.

'Secondly, in less than 48 hours from the Board meeting, minutes have been drafted, and have been personally handed over to me, by a special messenger from your office, on your instructions. This is also unprecedented, and I fail to understand, what is the hurry about!

'I am enclosing herewith e-mails sent to K. Sethuraman/ Surendra Pipara, which are self explanatory, for your information and appropriate action, since the additional agenda items may have been drafted by you, and this has been done without any discussion with me and without my express consent. The draft minutes mention that the Board discussed this matter, voted and unanimously approved with MDA abstaining from this resolution.

'I am clear that there was no discussion, and the question of vote, and passing the appropriate resolution thus does not even arise. Please appropriately correct your minutes and send them to me for my perusal.'

Finally, when the draft minutes remained unchanged, he wrote yet another long e-mail to Mukesh. This was his last attempt to correct what he perceived was wrong.

Anil to Mukesh, 30 July 2004, 09.58 p.m.: 'This is in continuation of my mail... and in response to the draft minutes received by me yesterday... from Vinod Ambani for my confirmation. Insofar as the item introduced on the supplemental agenda (now item No. 17 on the Draft Minutes) is concerned, I have already pointed out that apart from a discussion on "constituting the Health, Safety and Environment Committee" (which itself lasted barely two minutes), no discussion whatsoever had taken place at the Board meeting on 27.7.2004 on this agenda item in relation to the redefining of the powers of various committees, executives, the CMD, Vice Chairman & MD, and the other executive directors... I am surprised to subsequently learn that many of the other outside directors and other staff were aware, and had been spoken to about this, prior to the Board meeting. Not only do I not agree with the proposal as framed, but it is very clear to me that the Draft Minutes are factually incorrect. They purport to record a decision in relation to a discussion that has never happened.

'From other matters which I am learning about, and looking to the undue haste with which this item is being attempted to be pushed through, I am concerned that there appears to be more than meets the eye. The approach being adopted is not only contrary to all norms of corporate governance, but is also neither in good faith, nor in the spirit in which such matters have been dealt with in our company, or the traditions from the time of our late DHA (Dhirubhai Hirachand Ambani). It is indeed a sorry state of affairs.

'I have always treated you with respect, and I am unable to understand why you are attempting to proceed in this manner without taking me into confidence. A matter of this magnitude, which affects not only our company, but also each of us, and all our domestic and international stakeholders, cannot be introduced in this manner through a supplementary agenda item, without due notice, and without giving adequate time to the Directors for consideration of the consequences and ramifications of such a major step. This is a matter requiring careful thought, deep consideration, appropriate discussions, and above all, mutual agreement, before it can proceed further... Accordingly, I would once again request and suggest that, pending a discussion between us, item No. 17 as above be put in abeyance, so that the existing status quo is not disturbed, without a full discussion, debate and agreement between us. If however, this is not acceptable to you, you will appreciate that, much against my desires and wishes, I will be left with no other choice but to record my dissent appropriately. I sincerely hope it will not come to that, and we will revert to our earlier system of consultations/discussions/ mutual consent.

'It pains me that two AGMs and over eight Board meetings have taken place in the absence of Pappa, and unfortunately, things have now come to such a pass, that, for no apparent reason, such an important and detrimental action is being proposed. I look forward to a constructive solution and your understanding and advice.'

Mukesh didn't reply to this e-mail. The draft minutes, as far as I know, were treated as final ones. Even Sethuraman and Vinod Ambani tried to wriggle out of the situation. Take a look at the two e-mails Sethuraman wrote to Anil. In the first (29 July 2004, 06.51 p.m.) he said: 'With due respect, Sir, I must clarify here that neither have I acted surreptitiously nor have I abstracted any papers from anybody. All papers which had been left on the table by Directors (on 27 July) were, as per normal practice, collected by my team, after conclusion of the Board Meeting.' In his second mail (30 July 2004, 05.58 p.m.), he was more explicit. 'Sir, in my capacity as one of the members of the secretarial team, I have always endeavoured to follow the instructions given to me... Sir, the draft minutes were being handled by VMA (Vinod Ambani). In regard to matters stated in paras 1 to 3 (of Anil's e-mail dated 29 July 2004), I may point out that in these matters the role of the Secretarial Department is limited and I refrain from making any comments.'

On 30 July 2004, 05.40 p.m., Vinod Ambani also distanced himself from the issue. 'In compliance with the instructions I received to personally oversee the functioning of the Secretarial Department and take appropriate measures to streamline its functioning, I have introduced a system which is to be hereafter followed in case of every Board meeting, of circulating the Minutes to all Directors when the deliberations at the Board Meeting are still fresh in their minds.

'These steps have accordingly been introduced and since I was to go out of town the draft minutes were prepared promptly and circulated. The draft minutes were prepared on the basis of the Agenda and it was my intention to correctly record the proceedings of the Board Meeting.'

Given Mukesh's non-reaction, and others' reluctance to interfere in the matter, Anil did what he threatened in his e-mail to Mukesh. He wrote an emotional and aggressive letter to Mukesh. He made his unhappiness official.

Anil to the Chairman and Managing Director, Reliance Industries Ltd, 25 October 2004: '... I have expressed my views on this subject, through nine communications exchanged with the Chairman, and RIL's Secretarial Department, within a span of just three days starting from 27 July 2004, the date of the last Board meeting... I have stated... that Item No. 17 in the draft minutes has not been correctly recorded... I have requested the Chairman to keep this item in abeyance for the following reasons:

1. Item No. 17 was introduced... without proper and due notice.
2. The supplementary agenda was introduced without my knowledge and/or consent, and keeping me completely in the dark...
3. ... I have subsequently learnt that some of the other RIL Directors, and several RIL employees, had been taken into confidence on the supplementary agenda, and the contents and objectives of the same...
4. ... Some of the other RIL Directors, to whom I later spoke, expressed surprise that I was not aware of this supplementary agenda item, and had not been consulted on the same...

5. The supplementary agenda item had a misleading title... (and) obscured the real purpose of the agenda item...
6. The relevant proposals on the substantial redefinition of the powers of the Managing Directors were available only in the fine print in an Annexure...
7. There were no discussions or deliberations at the Board meeting, on this very substantial matter... as incorrectly stated in the minutes.
8. ... the proposed redefinition of powers of the Managing Directors, reflected a substantial and material variation of the equation as has existed in RIL for the past more than two decades, and this clearly required intensive discussion and consideration of the Board of Directors, based on full facts and circumstances being presented to the Board. None of this has happened.
9. This issue... is a matter of great importance, vitally affecting the corporate governance structure of the company...
10. The minutes incorrectly state that after discussions, all Directors (other than the CMD, who did not participate) unanimously approved of the resolution. The fact is that there were no discussions, and there was no vote, and the question of the resolution being passed unanimously thus does not arise...
12. I have also been legally advised that the proposed redefinition of powers... is not in accordance with law, and is in conflict with the provisions of the Companies Act, 1956...
16. It is also evident that the draft minutes were kept prepared in advance of the Board meeting, because there was no

adequate time for the Secretarial Department to prepare the draft after the conclusion of the meeting, and obtain signatures of several directors on the same day!... Regrettably... almost ninety days, after my second e-mail to the CMD, and my personal discussions with several directors, and their interventions in turn with the CMD, I have not received any acknowledgement, much less any response, from him to my aforesaid e-mails. Instead, it has been communicated to me on the CMD's behalf that the matter is final, and cannot be altered... It is my firm view that RIL should abide by the highest standards of corporate governance, and this should first be reflected at proceedings of our Board of Directors.'

No one listened to Anil. No one really cared. The RIL board seemed to have behaved like a rubber stamp, siding with Mukesh on this issue. Until then, the two brothers had shared almost equal powers in all respects. Now, Mukesh was changing the equation and the board was not even discussing or debating the pros and cons of such a crucial decision. The minutes of the next board meeting noted: 'Shri Anil D. Ambani, Vice Chairman and Managing Director, expressed his views relating to Item No. 17 of the Minutes of the meeting held on 27 July 2004 and placed a letter dated 25 October 2004 addressed by him to the Chairman and Managing Director on table. The letter was read out by Shri Anil D. Ambani to the Board. The Board considered the letter and noted the views of Shri Anil D. Ambani and his dissent to Item No. 17 of the Minutes. After discussions, the Board decided not to accede to the request made by Shri Anil D. Ambani...

The Board while noting the letter... took the same on record, confirmed the proceedings as recorded and noted the minutes of the meeting held on 27 July 2004, as circulated and tabled.'

That was it. The Board acquiesced. Mukesh won. And Anil was the loser.

Once the whole issue of the July board meeting became known, the Mukesh camp denied that Item No. 17 had curtailed Anil's powers or that it had changed the power structure between the two brothers within RIL. According to Mukesh's advisors, it had only institutionalized a system that is normally prevalent in professional organizations across the globe. Anil was only overreacting. He was behaving like a petulant child. He was getting emotional about it. A few days later, the Mukesh camp issued a note that spelt out the 'role of CEO and the reasons to redefine powers of Executive Chairman (Mukesh).' It was a strong counter to the issues that Anil had raised through his letters and e-mails about Item No. 17. It gave a spin that even Anil found difficult to refute. It talked of the role of the Chairman from the time the late Dhirubhai became one. It said Mukesh had to perform the same responsibilities as Dhirubhai.

'Across the globe it is the Chairman and the Chief Executive Officer of a Company who has all the powers of general management of the business of the company... It is also the practice that one or more Vice Chairmen of the Board shall be chosen... who shall be accountable to the Chief Executive Officer. This practice is followed in leading companies, such as General Electric Company, etc.

'Over the past three decades (since the time of Dhirubhai), the Executive Chairman has overall authority of the management of the business of the company and the Executive Vice Chairman and Wholetime Directors being accountable to the Executive Chairman carried/carry out the activities assigned by or orders made by the Executive Chairman from time to time. This had been the practice followed in RIL even when S/Sri Ramnikbhai Ambani and N.H. Ambani were Executive Directors and Sri Dhirubhai Ambani was the Executive Chairman... Both Sri Mukesh D. Ambani and Anil D. Ambani despite being Managing Directors reported to Executive Chairman, Sri Dhirubhai H. Ambani. This practice was consistently followed until the demise of Sri Dhirubhai Ambani.' So would be the case now that Mukesh had donned that role.

'Thus, the resolution passed by the Board of Directors on 27 July 2004 meeting is more of (sic) clarificatory in nature and is (sic) in no way changed or altered the hitherto practice followed by the Company in the last several years even when the founder Sri Dhirubhai H. Ambani was managing the affairs of the company.'

But why was it necessary to issue such clarifications? Why now? Why behind Anil's back?

For a long time, Mukesh had been uneasy about Anil. He had misgivings about the younger brother's professionalism, business acumen and sense of corporate strategy. Mukesh thought Anil went a bit overboard, both in his personal and professional life. And a number of Anil's decisions could – and did – end up hurting the interests of RIL, its board and its shareholders.

The most obvious one was Anil's move to join politics. On 16 June 2004, he filed the nomination papers for the Rajya

Sabha as an independent candidate from Lucknow. The same day the Samajwadi Party, led by Mulayam Singh Yadav, announced its support for Anil Ambani. Amar Singh SP's general secretary, said his party had the strength to get six members elected to the Rajya Sabha. As the party had announced five of them, Anil now would be their sixth.

I was intrigued by some of the photographs that appeared in the newspapers the next day. One of them showed MP and former film actress Jayaprada greeting Jaya Bachchan after the latter had filed her nomination papers as an SP candidate. Jayaprada was on Jaya's left, on her right was Mulayam Singh Yadav. Lurking just behind Jaya, with his eyes staring somewhere towards the horizon, was none other than Anil Ambani. There was another one. Anil sitting and filling up the nomination forms; his wife, Tina, on his right talking to someone on her mobile; Jaya Bachchan on his left submitting her papers; a smiling Jayaprada watching the action from behind; and a bored Subroto Roy, chieftain of the Sahara group, looking intently at Anil. A third one showed Anil taking the blessings of and touching the feet of the former HRD minister and senior BJP leader, Murli Manohar Joshi. Earlier, there had been other photographs that did not go well with the image of the conservative Ambanis. Dhirubhai was rarely photographed with politicians. Mukesh would only be seen with them at public functions where several dignitaries were present. Anil was different. He openly hobnobbed with politicians, middlemen and celebrities. There were several photographs of Anil either together or individually with Subroto Roy, Amar Singh, Amitabh Bachchan and Mulayam Singh Yadav.

Mukesh was upset by all this. He believed that although the twain does meet consistently, politics and business should not be seen to mix publicly. Mukesh was also of the view that the Ambanis should not reveal their personal wealth. That is what happened when Anil filed the Rajya Sabha nomination papers. Since the Election Commission had forced all candidates to disclose their wealth, Anil had to do so too. And what came out was quite sensational. Anil himself owned jewellery worth Rs 27.21 crore, his wife Tina owned jewellery worth nearly Rs 65 crore. The couple together had investments of over Rs 160 crore, and Anil had other assets worth Rs 90 crore.

For the conservative Ambanis, such disclosures were disgraceful. Why do it? What was the need to join politics if one was forced to reveal personal wealth? What was the point of all this? As one of Mukesh's friend told me: 'Mukesh was never comfortable with Anil's proximity to Amar Singh and Subroto Roy. And when Anil joined politics, Mukesh was quite upset.'

For Mukesh the last straw came when he learnt about Anil's nomination in the newspapers. (Mukesh has always claimed that neither he nor the RIL board knew about Anil's decision to become an MP.) Anil had done this without seeking his advice. As the note, which was circulated by Mukesh's camp to clarify the redefinition of powers between the two brothers, noted: 'Sri Anil D. Ambani became a member of the Rajya Sabha without any communication to Sri Mukesh D. Ambani nor the matter was informed to the Board of Directors before filing the papers...'

I asked Tony about it. He explained: 'Anil filed his papers at the behest of his mother. She was interested that Anil should join politics. He does not do anything without informing his mother. Even during this public fight with Mukesh, his mother has been aware of all the moves in advance. Nothing had been done without her knowledge, consent and blessings. Anyway, the decision to join politics was a personal one, and there was no need to inform the RIL board about it. It had no business implications.'

After Mukesh's camp alleged that the elder brother had no inkling about Anil's political plans, the other side issued a clarification. 'As far as the filing of nomination for Rajya Sabha is concerned... the press release issued by Anil Ambani on the date of his nomination is attached and is self-explanatory.' The press release stated: 'It will be my honour and privilege to make my humble contribution to the development of India as an economic superpower and the fast-track progress of the state of Uttar Pradesh, in accordance with my late father's desire and wishes.' It added: 'With the blessings of Lord Shiva, the blessings of my late father Dhirubhai Ambani, the blessings and support of my dear mother Kokilaben, and support of all members of the Ambani family, well-wishers and friends, it is my privilege and honour to have filed my nomination papers as an independent candidate for the Rajya Sabha...' So, did Mukesh know, or was he unaware – as his aides stated in their explanatory notes? There had to be something more to this issue.

Months later, when I was chatting with one of the FoA, I got some new insights into Anil's decision to join politics. 'Look at the entire context. Anil was battling his brother for a slice of the Reliance pie. He was alone, with only a handful of people on his side – whether you considered the RIL board, senior Reliance employees, or even his relatives (like the Meswanis). The odds were clearly against him. He needed friends, powerful ones who could help him in the fight. He needed people who could pressure his elder brother to give in and agree to an equitable split. Becoming a Rajya Sabha member was one way to achieve that objective.' The argument made sense. Mukesh controlled RIL, for he and AJ controlled the investment firms through which the Ambani family stake in the flagship was held. Through RIL, Mukesh controlled other group companies in which RIL had majority or substantial stakes. In such a scenario, all loyalties – internally and externally – shifted towards the seemingly winning horse, Mukesh.

But the MP episode riled Mukesh. In addition, there were also a couple of business decisions that convinced Mukesh that his younger brother was on the wrong track. One of these was Anil's intent to bid for tenders pertaining to the government's move to privatize some of the Indian airports. The Mukesh camp's note on redefinition of powers, which was issued once the details of the July 2004 RIL board meeting became public, stated: 'In response to an e-mail dated 29 June 2004 sent by Sri Anil D. Ambani with respect to filing of form of expression of interest for privatization of airports, Sri Mukesh D. Ambani did not approve of the proposal. Sri Anil D. Ambani responded that he was not seeking Sri Mukesh D. Ambani's approval but only wanted to keep Sri Mukesh D. Ambani informed of what he was planning to do.' Anil, according to the Mukesh camp, was going off on a tangent. He was taking independent business decisions without Mukesh's consent. He was risking Reliance group's future by refusing to discuss his business proposals with family members or the RIL Board.

Anil's response was curt. 'The filing of the form of expression of interest for privatization of airports was done by a Reliance Energy SPV called Reliance Airport Developers. The proposal required no financial commitments from RIL nor were any RIL resources used for the same.' When I asked Amitabh about it, his reply too was categorical: 'The airport project required just Rs 2000 crore. And it was only the bid stage; there were no financial commitments to be made at that time. And if Mukesh was so upset about it, why didn't he take it up with the RIL Board? It's a red herring.' But there was a flaw in this argument. RIL owned a major stake in Reliance Energy. As Anil had admitted, he was appointed by the RIL board to take charge of Reliance Energy. Thus, any business decisions taken by Reliance Energy should have involved RIL.

However, there was another project that became a bone of contention between the two brothers. It was one that convinced Mukesh that Anil's business strategy was questionable, while Anil thought that his elder brother was purposely trying to derail his ambitious plans. It was the breaking point, the point of no return.

On 26 December 2003, Arun Mishra, Chairman and Managing Director of Uttar Pradesh Power Corporation, made a sensational announcement. He told journalists that Reliance Industries Ltd planned to set up a 2000-3000 MW power plant in western Uttar Pradesh. The proposed project, he added, could result in an investment of nearly Rs 8000 crore.

'We have already shown them some sites in western UP. The company is examining different locations and we expect the proposal to assume concrete shape soon. They have indicated a requirement of about 2500 acres of land,' Mishra told *Hindu Business Line*.

UP had been trying to woo private power producers for some time. The state had announced a new policy to give incentives to private investors. These included interest-free loans equivalent to the entry tax and state trade tax, a tax moratorium of between seven and twelve years, land at acquisition costs and waiver of stamp duty. 'We are encouraging private sector power producers to use the liberalized norms under the new policy to enter all segments – production, distribution and transmission,' added Mishra.

Almost a month later, on 27 January 2004, Reliance issued a press release to make it official. Anil Ambani said the Dadri (UP) project, with an investment outlay of over Rs 10,000 crore, would be the largest gas-based power generating facility globally. The fuel – natural gas – for the plant would be 'sourced from Reliance group's Dhirubhai gas fields in the Krishna-Godavari basin off the coast of Andhra Pradesh. The fields... represent the largest discovery of natural gas in the world in the year 2002-03... Sri Anil D. Ambani dedicated the project as a tribute to the vision of his late father, Sri Dhirubhai Ambani who always believed that India's emergence as an economic superpower lay in the availability of reliable, clean and green power at a competitive cost... The Reliance group... was committed to fulfilling the vision... by playing a meaningful role in the development of this basic and extremely important infrastructure in the country.'

At the peak of the Ambani fight, Mukesh hurled charges against Anil relating to the power project. Anil had announced the project without the consent of the RIL board. He announced RIL's commitments to supply gas for the project and that Reliance Energy would implement the project without the RIL Board's approval. Mukesh said that at a personal level he too wasn't aware of the ambitious project.

Anil retaliated. He said the RIL Board had approved the project on 29 January 2004. The Board decided that RIL could invest up to Rs 5000 crore in generation, transmission and distribution projects of Reliance Energy. Here's what *The Times of India* wrote in support of Anil Ambani on the Dadri project: '... RIL had committed to investing Rs 3500 crore, However, the entire amount was not required by REL (Reliance Energy), which raised Rs 1100 crore from Indian and overseas institutional investors and another Rs 800 crore through foreign currency convertible bonds. By early April (2004), RIL's equity commitment was reckoned to be about Rs 1,500 crore. Total equity for the project was about Rs 3000 crore, the rest would be financed by debt.

'"There was no ambiguity. Every director in RIL (including Mukesh) was aware of the details of the project and had even approved investments. Where is the question of unilateral decision-making?" says a director who was present at RIL's 29 January board meeting that approved the Dadri investment. The approval came after the two brothers had discussed the project threadbare for over a month. As early as the third week of December 2003, approvals were sought from the UP government for the project.'

Once again, there was a catch. The RIL board approved the project on 29 January 2004. But Anil had officially announced it on 27 January 2004, or two days before the meeting. Technically, he had jumped the gun. Technically, he had taken a unilateral decision. Technically, he was in the wrong. Worse, Mukesh never did like anything about the project. As days went by, the elder brother felt that the project's location was chosen merely because of Anil's proximity to the Samajwadi Party. And he thought RIL would be better off selling gas to outsiders at more profitable rates, rather than to Reliance Energy. Going by the bad experiences of several MNC power developers, Mukesh decided there was no need for the Reliance group to undertake a mega project that was fraught with too many risks.

Anil saw it as Mukesh's way to spite him. This was Anil's big moment. This was his chance to come out of the shadow of his elder brother. This was an opportunity to prove to the world that he too could be a builder. That he could implement mega projects. That he could do what his brother had done at Jamnagar. If Mukesh could successfully build the world's largest greenfield refinery, Anil would build the world's largest gas-based power plant. Once the Dadri project went onstream, no one would ever suspect Anil's credibility as an entrepreneur.

The younger brother was extremely upset when RIL started going slow on committing gas for the Dadri project. Initially, the supply was to start from 2006. Later, RIL said it might take an additional one or two years for it to happen. To Anil, it seemed that RIL was deliberately scuttling his dream project. It seemed Mukesh didn't want him to succeed.

RIL's explanation was that there were problems with turning on the gas. When I spoke to Nikhil Meswani in Mumbai, he told me this: 'I personally handled all the necessary government approvals required before we could start pumping out gas from the Krishna-Godavari fields. We faced a lot of delays in getting the permissions. You know how the bureaucracy works and the number of clearances that are required. It was not our intent to delay supplies. It just took more time than we had envisaged. That's all.'

But this didn't wash with Anil. He thought that while Mukesh was pumping in thousands of crores of rupees in Reliance Infocomm, he was unwilling to help finance his project. That's why the fight between the brothers escalated.

6
Anatomy of a Split

> *All war is deception.*
> — *The Art of War* by Sun Tzu
>
> *It's true even about the initiatives to smoke the peace pipe.*
> — Ambani interpretation

On 18 June 2005, I was enjoying my long-awaited holiday in Sikkim. That morning, the clouds were wafting into my room through the open window, it was drizzling and slightly chilly. It was a perfect setting for a holiday. The Ambanis were nowhere on my radar.

And then I switched on the TV, and nearly hit the low ceiling. The two brothers were about to announce a truce; the RIL board was meeting to consider and clear the division agreement that had been accepted by both brothers. Although it was expected, I didn't think it would happen so fast. By that evening, I got the details of the split. RIL and IPCL to Mukesh; RCIL, Reliance Infocomm, Reliance Energy and Reliance Capital to Anil; a non-competing clause between the two brothers for five years; and there was more.

As I digested what signified an end to a battle that I had been closely following for seven months – and also an end to a legacy that I had been obsessed with for nearly two decades – I felt a tug somewhere. There was a sense of relief that this story was finally over and that my book would be ready soon. At the same time, I was also transported into the recent past, as I remembered all the twists, turns, U-turns, and tangential take offs that I had witnessed on the way to the brothers' final compromise. It was a tale of truths, half-truths and white lies.

As usual, 6 January 2005, a Thursday, had been a busy one – my magazine goes to bed every Thursday – and I reached home around midnight. Out of habit, I switched on the TV and started surfing news channels. As usual, I was looking for the latest in the ongoing Ambani saga.

I was stunned when I saw the news flashes on Aaj Tak – Anil and Mukesh to part ways, Anil and Mukesh to split equitably… Then I saw the faces – Pranjal Sharma, the channel's business editor, and Prabhu Chawla, its editorial head, involved in an intense discussion.

My heart sank. I had been closely following the Ambani story for nearly eight weeks, catching every twist and turn in that corporate melodrama. And now, our rival had scooped the biggest story about the details of the actual split between the two brothers. (*India Today* and *Outlook* had been fierce competitors since the latter's entry in the newsmagazine segment.) Worse, I was not in any position to react. It was too late for me to do an article for the current issue as it was going to press the same night.

Not knowing what else to do, I increased the volume. Prabhu apparently had all the details. He knew that the two

Ambanis had decided to go separate ways. K.V. Kamath, the ICICI chief and a close family friend, who had been acting as the honest broker and mediator, had helped in arriving at the division formula. Mother Kokilaben had given her blessings to the agreement that was finalized on 28 December 2004, when all the family members (including the two daughters and their husbands) had gathered at Sea Wind for the late Dhirubhai's birth anniversary. And Prabhu had all the numbers relating to the ratio in which both the family's holdings in RIL and the various businesses would be apportioned between the various members.

The news channel shifted to interviewing corporate lawyers and CAs on whether the formula could work, whether there were legal issues involved, whether the shareholders' consent was required. Prabhu cleared all the doubts. Apparently, he had it from the horses' mouths that there would be no problems, no hassles, and no bottlenecks. It was all a family matter and the members had sorted it out amicably. No outsider could interfere with it, either legally or otherwise. It was a foolproof deal.

Shattered as I was, I called up Tony.

'What's Aaj Tak saying?' I asked, my voice all edgy.

'I got calls from journalists asking me the same thing. I am in the car and haven't seen TV. What is Prabhu saying?' he asked.

I gave him the bare details and wanted to know if it was true. 'I don't know. There's some deal which has happened, but I don't know the details. I'll have to check because I think Prabhu's numbers may be wrong.'

'Where's Anil Bhai right now. Can I speak to him?'

'Right now, he must be thousands of metres up in the air, he just caught a Delhi-Mumbai flight.'

That depressed me further. Anil was in Delhi today. He must have met Prabhu and briefed him about the deal. The details had to come from one of the Ambanis. 'Did Prabhu meet him today?' I demanded to know.

'Alam, this hasn't come from our side. Rest assured about that. It must be Mukesh's aides who have probably leaked it to Prabhu. I know Prabhu spoke to Mukesh Bhai today. Yes, Anil met Prabhu in a hotel lobby. I was there and I can tell you the conversation they had. Prabhu asked Anil Bhai to appear in *Seedhi Baat* (a weekly interview-based show Prabhu hosts in Aaj Tak) and said he won't ask any questions relating to the two brothers. Anil refused. There was no other discussion.'

Obviously, I wasn't convinced. So, I called Amitabh. 'Have you seen Aaj Tak?'

'No, I haven't. I'm out. But I have got calls. What's Prabhu saying?'

Once again, I gave him a quick summary. 'So, is it true?' I was desperate to know.

'I don't know. But I don't think so. Alam, just relax. I know your deadline is today but let me assure you that you don't have to do a story on it. There's nothing like that.'

Amitabh's Delhi-based colleague was admitting to a deal. But Amitabh was denying it. What were these two guys up to? Why were they talking contradictory language? And why did Amitabh not want me to write anything about what was the biggest business story of the year? Why was he asking me to relax and forget it, while Tony was saying the opposite? Didn't they realize I could lose my job?

My next few calls were to members of the other camp. I called Anand Jain. He didn't pick up his phone. I tried Nikhil Meswani. He was probably sleeping. I was getting jittery. No one was confirming the deal. But Prabhu was so cocksure about it. He had that smirk on his face, he knew every single business journalist would be jealous of him.

Finally, I spoke to my immediate boss. For the third time in ten minutes, I told him what Prabhu was saying and that Anil's advisors were denying it or feigning lack of knowledge. My managing editor said we couldn't do anything about it anyway; we were too late and the issue was practically closed. So I just continued watching Aaj Tak, getting more depressed and, finally, at three, I went to sleep.

My dreams were all about the Ambanis. I dreamt about the December meeting between the Ambani family members, of how my boss was angry at my having missed the story, of my colleague telling me that *India Today* magazine would also not have it this week. Why? Because Prabhu had got it on a Thursday, and the magazine sends its final pages to the press on Wednesdays. But what if Prabhu had deliberately delayed airing it by a day. That way, he could ensure that *Outlook* couldn't do anything about it, and *India Today* would still have it as cover... As you can guess, I slept badly that night.

Fortunately for me, *India Today* didn't have it as the cover. In fact, it had a piece similar to ours – *Outlook* had a two-pager on 'All the Boss' (Mukesh's) Men' and *India Today* had a two-page profile on Anand Jain, Mukesh's main advisor.

The next few days, on an almost daily basis, there were more surprises. Courtesy the same advisors that I had been talking to from the two camps. It was as if everyone was either lying or telling half-truths. Either they didn't know, or they were deliberately confusing the hell out of journalists. In this Ambani battle, I started believing in the age-old maxim: listen to everyone, believe no one.

The Mukesh camp denied any knowledge about any deal. Anil's advisors initially feigned ignorance, then categorically stated that there was a deal, and later backtracked from that stance. They said that the negotiation process had been initiated and that Kamath had been entrusted with the task of suggesting options on how the brothers could amicably divide the operational assets of the Reliance group. After a while, Mukesh's aides too stopped denying the role of Kamath as the mediator. All these flip-flops happened in less than a week after Aaj Tak's so-called exclusive.

Hours after Prabhu went on air with the news about the Ambani agreement, a rival news channel claimed it wasn't true. The latter said there was no deal. The same day ICICI issued a denial saying Kamath wasn't involved in the Ambani affairs. Kamath personally issued another letter stating he wasn't advising the Ambanis on the division of the group. Less than forty-eight hours after Tony and Amitabh had given me different versions of the same event, they started singing the same tune. Both now said there was a deal and Prabhu's details were correct. According to them, Kamath's denial was expected – 'What else could he have said? He couldn't have shouted about it from the rooftop.'

At the December family meeting, the two chorused, everyone was present – Kokilaben, Mukesh, Anil, Dipti, Nina, Shyam and Dattaraj. The formula devised by Kamath, who was aided by the two sons-in-law, was placed on the table; Kokilaben and her two sons had studied it earlier. Kokilaben said she was fine with it. So did Mukesh and Anil. The two sisters had no problems. The two sons-in-law never had any interest in the Reliance group; they had their own profitable empires (albeit much smaller) and were satisfied with the money they were making.

Anil's advisors told me that for the first time, each family member agreed on the modalities of the division and that Mukesh and Anil should go their separate ways and build their own respective business fiefdoms.

When I met Anil, along with Amitabh, in his Mumbai office a few days after Aaj Tak aired news of the deal, he reiterated the details. The family's holdings in RIL would be divided in the following ratio – 30 per cent each to Kokilaben, Mukesh and Anil with 5 per cent each to Dipti and Nina. The business operations would be divided 'fairly and equitably', in a ratio that was close to 50:50 in terms of either assets, revenues or cashflows. 'It could be 60:40, but not as unfair as 70:30 or 80:20 in Mukesh's favour,' clarified Amitabh. The division would include clear-cut and separate ownership of the various companies so that there were no problems with future inheritances. 'Mukesh's children will run those owned by their father, and Anil's the ones that would fall in their dad's lap,' piped in Amitabh. Neither of the brothers would interfere in each other's operations. Mukesh and Anil would live happily thereafter.

There seemed to be a few problems with what Anil and Amitabh were saying. In terms of assets and revenues, RIL accounted for 80-90 per cent of the Reliance group. When one looked at cashflows, the percentage would certainly be higher. So how would the Ambanis carve up the empire in an equitable fashion? Would they break up RIL? And what would happen to cross-holdings – the stakes that RIL had in other group firms? It seemed quite complicated.

'This could be done easily. A few businesses – like gas exploration – could be spun off from RIL and transferred to Anil; he could be given other companies. RIL's holdings in firms that go to Anil could either be transferred to separate firms where RIL shareholders would be issued shares in the same ratio as RIL's stake, or the holdings could be demerged and distributed to RIL investors in the same ratio as existing holding pattern,' explained Amitabh. What he meant by demerger was that RIL shareholders could own that stake directly in Reliance Energy, if the company went to Anil. For example, since RIL held 42 per cent stake in Reliance Energy, the Ambani family, which held a combined 46.67 per cent in RIL, would be offered 19.60 per cent in Reliance Energy, that is 46.67 per cent of 42 per cent. The same would happen in case RIL's stake in Reliance Energy was transferred to a separate company or a special purpose vehicle.

Amitabh insisted that this would not involve too many legal or regulatory problems. It would be a clean, transparent and an easy way to execute a split. It did sound like a great idea, and I went back convinced that the Ambanis had found a solution to end their feud. But then, there was another surprise awaiting me, when I met Anand Jain the next day.

He went ballistic. 'Reports of a deal are without any foundation. This is smoke without any fire at all. There was no meeting on 28 December, there was no agreement, there was no deal,' said AJ, who's not known to get too excited about issues. He leant forward and asked: 'Tell me why is he (Anil) spreading such rumours? Tell me, because I am confused.' And he proceeded to answer the question: 'Probably his camp is only trying to find a new twist every week to keep journalists busy.' Later, I came to know that AJ had echoed similar statements to several dailies and TV channels, which had, therefore, decided to underplay the agreement story.

By this time, my head was in a spin. Was there a deal or not? Who was speaking the truth? Or were both camps lying outright or telling half-truths? I nudged AJ a bit more. 'What's the evidence that there's no deal?' He immediately pointed out more discrepancies in Anil's version of the event. 'If a meeting had been held between family members that December Tuesday, then why did Anil resign from his IPCL's posts the next week? In his resignation letter, why did he criticize me and say it was below his dignity to work with me? Doesn't Anil know that whenever two parties have decided to talk and discuss, there's a cooling-off period when no party is supposed to talk about it unless the deal is signed and sealed? Why did Anil go public with the formula?'

AJ had a point. And then AJ came up with another of his well-thought out arguments. 'Tell me, did Anil tell you he has met and spoken to Mukesh?' I said no. In fact, Anil told me that the two brothers discussed the split formula through their mother. They both had a one-on-one with Kokilaben. 'If that's true, how can Anil claim there's an agreement when he hasn't even directly discussed it with his brother?' questioned AJ.

Nothing made sense any more. The media too was divided. The journalists who were close to Anil kept projecting the fact that a deal had been struck between the two brothers. But those close to Mukesh said the opposite. Aaj Tak, meanwhile, decided to maintain a stony silence after the initial excitement, and distanced itself from the so-called deal exclusive. The news channel just stopped saying anything about an agreement between the two Ambani brothers.

I had no option but to talk to the other side about the observations made by Mukesh's A-Team. Anil's B-Team said they were totally baffled by AJ's denial of the agreement. 'Why are they lying to you?' As usual, before I could answer it, they suggested a possibility. 'They are posturing to extract the best deal; one that would go totally in Mukesh's favour. Can they really deny that the family was together at the Ambanis' Sea Wind residence on 28 December?' AJ had a simple answer to it. 'The family did meet, as it was Dhirubhai's birth anniversary. But nothing was discussed. As you said, the two brothers didn't even talk to each other.'

It was an impossible situation. I didn't know whom to believe any more. Anil was insisting there was a deal. AJ was claiming there was none. Finally, on deadline day that Thursday (13 January 2005), I got an inkling of the facts when Anil's advisors did a virtual U-turn. Yes, the family did meet on 28 December 2004. Yes, the members did agree to initiate a process to split the Reliance group. And they had asked family friend, Kamath, to do a valuation of the group's assets and give a report within four weeks. But they now said that no final agreement had been reached on how to split the group.

Once the ICICI chief submitted his report, a formal

process would be initiated to carve up the empire between the two brothers and Kamath would suggest options on how best to achieve this objective. (To re-emphasize Kamath's role, Anil's camp leaked information the following week about Anil's meeting with Kamath at the latter's residence on Sunday, 16 January. Later, Tony told me that the fact that the two had met was proof that Kamath was involved in the division process.)

Even this version of events seemed fraught with problems. For, I got the impression that Mukesh did not want to give up either RIL or Reliance Infocomm. 'Only the elder brother had been involved in the telecom venture since its inception in 1999. Anil had not contributed anything to Infocomm. Unlike in other companies, even Dhirubhai, while he was alive, wasn't on Infocomm's board. Of the Ambanis, only Mukesh was on its board. It was Mukesh's baby. So, how do you expect Mukesh to give it up?' questioned AJ.

Mukesh's key advisor had similar thoughts about RIL. 'Who ran RIL? Mukesh. Who controlled the flagship? Mukesh. Who did the late Dhirubhai annoint as the future chairman? Mukesh, as he was appointed the vice chairman, while Anil was still only a managing director. Who had the complete support of the RIL board? Mukesh. Who had set up all the mega projects implemented by RIL? Mukesh. So, how could he just give it to Anil?' There was also no question about splitting RIL, as the company's board had made it clear that it would continue to run as an integrated energy company.

To Anil, it seemed like a facile argument. To him, it seemed RIL was suffering from a stock market disease, which he termed as, 'conglomerate discount'. Since the Ambani flagship was operating in diverse areas – from exploration to telecom – the stock market pundits didn't quite understand the mechanics of its operations. They couldn't figure out the underlying value of the sum of all these seemingly diverse parts of its businesses. That's why the RIL stock had underperformed the Sensex, especially in the last two years. The markets were, therefore, discounting RIL. Given this context, it may not be such a bad idea for RIL to shed a few of its components and focus on core areas.

A study in the US, covering a 25-year period till 1988, found that the stocks of spun-off companies outperformed their industry peers as well as the Standard & Poor 500 (the New York Stock Exchange market index) by about 10 per cent annually during the first three years of the formation of the new company. Even the parent firm managed to do well – outperforming their competitors in the same sectors by over 6 per cent during the same three-year period. In India, the best example has been the recent hiving off of the cement division by L&T. The spinoff unlocked L&T's inherent value, as the stock jumped 75 per cent from Rs 500 to Rs 875. The new cement company, UltraTech Cemco, was quoted recently at Rs 295, a reasonable value in the sector.

As I pursued the Ambanis in a bid to understand the significance of – and the truth behind – what the family members and their advisors were saying, it struck me that Mukesh was trying hard to step into his father's shoes. For there were occasions when one saw shades of Dhirubhai in Mukesh's behaviour. (In toto, Mukesh was quite different from his father, and Anil seemed closer to Dhirubhai, but Mukesh seemed to have learnt his lessons well.)

Early on in the Ambani fight, on 24 November 2004, Mansingh L. Bhakta resigned from the RIL's board. It was quite a blow as Bhakta had been a close family friend and had been an RIL director for twenty-seven years. A senior partner in the Mumbai-based law firm, Kanga and Co, he had written a letter stating his resignation was due to his advancing age. He also told mediapersons that the current rivalry between Mukesh and Anil had nothing to do with his decision. But to his close friends, Bhakta said he was disgusted with the manner in which the two brothers were fighting. 'What their father built in two decades, they would destroy in two weeks,' he told them. To outsiders, Bhakta's resignation implied the RIL Board was not completely behind Mukesh.

The next afternoon, Mukesh went to Bhakta's office. This was quintessential Dhirubhai, who would not allow ego or arrogance to come in the way of finding quick solutions to crises. As someone close to Dhirubhai said, 'This is exactly what the patriarch would have done. This was Dhirubhai's way of disarming the other party, making them feel important, and wooing them to his side.' Mukesh did the same. He went to Kanga & Co's Mumbai office, located in the crowded Fort area, walked up the cramped and dirty stairs to the first floor, and met Bhakta for nearly two hours.

Coincidentally, I was there at Kanga & Co's office at the same time. I had gone with a couple of photographers in an attempt to talk to Bhakta. We were told he was in a meeting. We had no idea who he was meeting. We waited for 30-odd minutes. As we were waiting in the reception area, a couple of employees rudely asked us to go away. 'Mr Bhakta won't be free today. There's no point for you to wait. You can call him tomorrow,' said one. We walked out of the office and were debating what to do while standing near the lift.

Suddenly, I saw *Outlook's* photographer, Atul Loke, running down the stairs. So did the *Indian Express* photographer, who was with us. Instinctively, I ran down too.

All I could see was a short, slightly bulky man hurrying down the stairs, followed by two men who behaved like security guards, followed by the two photographers. Downstairs, I realized it was Mukesh. The two photographers went berserk, clicking away with their digital cameras. There was no way I could squeeze past the two securitymen. I just observed how Mukesh, realizing the photographs would be in the newspapers the next day, broke into a smile. There was no way he was going to let the world know that he was frustrated, or angry, or under pressure. He would show the world that things were normal. I was surprised that Mukesh's car was not waiting at the entrance; in fact, he walked seventy to eighty steps to the vehicle parked at one corner of the road.

Hours later, the news was on the agency tickers. Bhakta had decided to take back his resignation. Mukesh had convinced him to stay on RIL's Board. It was a corporate coup. Yet again, Anil, who thought Bhakta's action would put pressure on his elder brother to come to the negotiating table, had lost out. The RIL Board was still behind Mukesh.

Similarly, Mukesh's behaviour at the ET award ceremony, as mentioned in the previous chapter, was a.k.a. Dhirubhai. The fact that he had walked up to Anil and shook hands with him during the height of their feud was meant to send a clear message to the public – that Mukesh was all humility and that he harboured no ill-feelings towards his younger brother despite the several allegations hurled by Anil against him. The patriarch would have been proud of Mukesh for this was something he himself would have done. As Sun Tzu said: 'Pretend inferiority and encourage his (the enemy's) arrogance.'

But Anil knew Sun Tzu's war philosophy better than his brother. He was more worried about Kamath's valuation and the options that he might suggest about the possible carve-up. And he was getting tense as Kamath's report had got delayed. It was finally given towards the end of February 2005, nearly a month late. Immediately, Anil's advisors worked overtime to give the right spin to journalists so that their version stood out.

Kamath submitted his report to Kokilaben in February 2005, and the mother gave it to her sons separately to study. Apart from valuing the group's assets, based on information tendered by both camps, the ICICI supremo provided options about the possible ways in which the empire could be divided between Mukesh and Anil. To do that, he studied recent business families' splits in the US and a few East Asian countries like Malaysia. Several experts helped him in the task – such as the well-known investment banker, Nimesh Kampani of JM Morgan Stanley. Kamath also had the blessings of the finance minister, P. Chidambaram.

(Kamath refused to comment even then. Only months later, in May 2005, he acknowledged his role in the Reliance affair. In an interview with Shekhar Gupta, Editor-in-Chief, *Indian Express*, which was aired on NDTV, he said that the problems between the Ambani brothers will be resolved because 'every family issue that I have seen finally gets settled'. He added he wasn't a mediator between them and that he could describe his role as that of 'helping two people communicate. I'd say it's a steady process of getting two people to communicate. And that's been going on. It's a large process. The stakes are very high. It's going on... Both talk to me. I talk to them. So the process is on.')

But the process was clearly a treacherous one. For Kamath had to deal with the sensitive and prickly issue in a 'fair and equitable' manner. It wouldn't be easy. Everything might be fair in war, but there was nothing fair when it came to ceasefire. There were only winners and losers and each side walked away with a feeling that it had got a raw deal. There were a number of landmines that Kamath had to negotiate during the peace process, even if they had been placed there recently.

James Lea, a professor at the University of North Carolina, said it succintly: 'I've found three simple words that cause a lot of the difficulties encountered by families in business. The first word is "mine"... The second one is "when"... The third... "fair"... I want to be fair to all the children is often the opening line in a family business tragedy.' What Lea meant by the 'third word' is that a patriarch can never be fair to all his siblings. He'll always have to make a choice and favour one over the others. To be unfair to the Ambanis, Kokilaben had said that last line to many of her friends and well-wishers. Anil too had told me that the split should be seemingly fair, which meant nearly half the assets should come to him. For Mukesh, fair meant that he should own, control and manage business entities that he had built single-handedly (which included RIL and Reliance Infocomm, or over 80-90 per cent of the group's revenues.)

Hence, there were difficulties with all the options that

Kamath had explored and mentioned in his February report. One of these was that of the two big firms, RIL should go to Mukesh and Reliance Infocomm to Anil. The rest could be divided fairly easily between the two – IPCL to Mukesh, and Reliance Energy and Reliance Capital to Anil. It suited neither. Mukesh had built Infocomm, and he did not want to part with his dream project. Anil knew that Infocomm's future was bright, only if RIL was willing to help it financially. Although the telecom venture had recently received a loan commitment of $750 million from foreign lenders, its viability was tied to RIL, the cash cow. That umbilical cord couldn't be cut too easily – as RIL had pumped in nearly Rs 18,000 crore in Infocomm at one point in time – and Anil would be uncomfortable if Mukesh held the scissors. For Mukesh could cut the financial cord and leave Infocomm in the lurch.

Another issue that was likely to create bad blood between Anil and Mukesh was the existing link between RIL and Reliance Infocomm. Although Anil wanted RIL to continue to help the telecom venture, he wanted this to happen on his own terms, not on Mukesh's. The reason: Anil had openly and publicly criticized the existing relationship between the two firms. If RIL's exposure in Infocomm was unfair while Mukesh was managing the telecom firm, how could it become fair if Anil got Infocomm as part of the ongoing settlement process?

As stated in a previous chapter, Anil felt RIL had paid a much higher price for its stake in RCIL, Infocomm's parent company, than what Mukesh and his friends had paid for their holdings in Reliance Infocomm. He had made it an ethical issue that RIL was being used as a milch cow to finance Mukesh's dreams. In another instance, RIL had pumped in

Rs 8,100 crore in preference shares at a premium of Rs 49 per share (face value: Re 1) in Infocomm while others – including RIL – had paid a mere Re 1 per share for their equity stakes.

Would he now arm-twist RIL to convert these preference shares into equity – as they were meant to be converted – at a lower premium than Rs 49 per share, even though RIL may belong exclusively to Mukesh in the future? But if he did that, Infocomm's equity base would get bloated – since a lower premium meant that more equity shares would be allotted to RIL – and threaten the viability of the telecom firm that would land in Anil's lap. Alternatively, if Anil decided that RIL should pay a higher premia to keep the equity base size under control, he could be accused of being unfair to RIL and its shareholders – a charge that he had hurled against Mukesh in the past. Finally, if he decided that Reliance Infocomm should return the money to RIL, as his advisors had hinted earlier, Anil would find it difficult to raise money to pay back Rs 8,100 crore, and that too at a time when Infocomm needed additional cash to finance its expansion. (After the split, Anil settled for a much lower premium of Rs 32 per share to be fair to RIL's shareholders.)

In March 2005, however, it was a classic Catch 22 situation. Anil had little idea how to wriggle out of it.

There was another catch and an important one too. Anil had to contend with his future in the power business, in case he got Reliance Energy. He had already announced the ambitious over Rs 10,000 crore gas-based power plant in Uttar Pradesh – the largest of its kind in the world. But its commissioning depended on two issues which would have to be decided by Mukesh. One, RIL had to finance the project as one of its promoters. Two, the proposed project's viability depended on confirmed – and sustained – gas commitments from RIL's Krishna-Godavari gas fields.

Would Mukesh agree to part with those fields, something that the RIL Board had refused to do? Would RIL's shareholders and institutional investors agree to such a transfer? Would Anil be satisfied with a verbal or a written commitment from RIL that it would support his power project, now that the two brothers had fought so bitterly? There were just too many question marks.

However, the overriding advantage of one of Kamath's options as per his February 2005 report – that is, to give RIL to Mukesh and Infocomm to Anil – was that it would push the brothers onto different strategic paths. With RIL and IPCL in his bag, Mukesh could aim to become the manufacturing magnate. And Anil, with his presence in sectors such as telecom, power and financial services, could be the services superstar.

In comparison, the other two options given by Kamath seemed unworkable. One was that most of the group firms – RIL, IPCL, RCIL and Reliance Infocomm – should go to Mukesh. Anil would be left with Reliance Energy and Reliance Capital. Since Anil was the clear loser in such a deal, he would be compensated with loads of cash – in return for his share of the family stake in both RIL and Reliance Infocomm (the 55 per cent that was held by Mukesh and Nita would be treated as belonging to the entire family, or belonging equally to both Mukesh and Anil). In his February report, Kamath stated that the 34.04 per cent stake, held by the Ambani family through hundreds of investment firms should be divided in a

30:30:30:10 ratio between mother Kokilaben, Mukesh, Anil, and the two sisters. Obviously, the money paid to Anil would be adjusted for RIL's stakes in the two companies that went to the younger brother.

The problem with this option was: how would Mukesh find cash running into thousands of crores of rupees to pay Anil? And would Anil remain satisfied with fledgling businesses and cash?

Kamath's third option was a red herring. It was one that would never work, not after what had happened in the past couple of years. This was that despite their differences, they could still work together in RIL. With the backdrop of hurt egos and personality clashes, even the best of friends agreed Mukesh and Anil would be unhappy together.

From the way I saw it at that time, there was only one way out: the option under which RIL went to Mukesh and Infocomm to Anil.

But even this option would require a number of issues to be thrashed out, apart from the ones mentioned above. A niggling subject would be about valuations – how best to value the cross-holdings in various group companies. If Anil had to get out of RIL, Mukesh had to pay a fair price for the younger brother's stake – and it had to be at a huge premia as Anil was giving up management control. The same logic would apply in case of Reliance Infocomm – Mukesh would demand a huge premia to get out of that firm since he too was giving up management control. Moreover, Infocomm was no longer a start-up and its business had to be valued at a higher price. Finally, the formula would have to be acceptable to both brothers vis-à-vis IPCL, Reliance Energy or Reliance Capital.

What they needed was an acceptable mediator who they could trust and listen to.

'They would need to depend on a few detached and objective family members to work out the details. Dipti's husband, Dattaraj Salgoacar, could be one such person as he was neither interested nor involved in Reliance. Although Nina's husband, Shyam Kothari, wasn't interested in being part of the Reliance empire, he did handle a portion of Reliance's broadband business in South India. So, he would not be acceptable. There were other friends like Kamath who could help sort out problems relating to valuations of group companies,' confided a family friend.

By end of March 2005, nearly a month after Kamath submitted his report, the negotiations sounded serious. This was different from the 28 December 2004 fiasco when the two sides agreed to disagree on whether there was a deal or not. I got the first hint when I called up Anand Jain. 'I am a finance guy. Now that the financial issues are no longer in the picture, I don't want to talk to the media. Talk to RIL's spokesperson. Please don't disturb me,' AJ banged the phone down, which was quite unlike him. Was this an indication that the time to hiss was over and now it was kiss, discuss and make up?

Indeed, there was another reason to believe something was up in the air. In January 2005, AJ had told me that the only way to gauge that a deal was being hatched was to watch out for that lull, that period when the two camps stopped talking to the media and instead started talking to each other. Indeed, throughout most of March and April 2005, the advisors on both sides seemed to have taken a break. Some didn't even take my calls, others were quietly planning their forthcoming holidays. (Remember, all of them had to cancel their New Year's plans because of the brothers' fallout.)

Still, my instincts told me something different. The House of Ambanis was built in haste – it became a Rs 100,000 crore empire in just over two decades. Reliance's competitors were destroyed at a frenetic pace. The ongoing Ambani vs Ambani script was written in a hurry, with the screenplay changing every day. But the split story could still be a long-winded one given the sensitive issues involved.

April 2005. The atmosphere at Reliance Infocomm's office at Navi Mumbai's Dhirubhai Ambani Knowledge Centre (DAKC) was sombre and serious. The employees were worried, they had no idea about their professional fate. For they had heard rumours that Infocomm may now be headed by Anil. Mukesh, who had fathered the project since its incubation had not visited DAKC in the recent past. Neither had the two strategic nerve centres, Anand Jain and Manoj Modi.

Of course, the senior managers had received feelers from the Mukesh camp. They had been gingerly asked whether they would like to stay with Mukesh, or move over to the other side. They had a choice. Since RIL had huge retail plans – to set up hundreds of petrol pumps across the country – their skills could be useful even if Infocomm went to Anil. Or they could stay back and work with Anil. The younger brother's aides told me they were getting calls from managers who were keen to emphasize their loyalties to Anil. Obviously, the managers had an inkling that Infocomm could go to Anil as part of one of Kamath's formulae. It was the mid-level employees who were in the dark. Many of them, and some of the senior managers, quit due to the uncertainty.

Only the most critical decisions were being taken. Infocomm seemed to be in limbo, as managers did not know who they had to really please – Mukesh & Co or Anil and his advisors. AJ, however, claimed that business was as usual. Once, when I casually asked him what he and Mukesh talked about these days, he said: 'We discuss business on a daily basis. There are so many decisions that have to be made everyday. We have to run the Reliance group too, Alam.'

But clearly, neither AJ nor Mukesh was spending too much time on Infocomm. Instead, it was Anil who was doing all the strategic thinking. For example, he met Pradip Baijal, the telecom regulator, to discuss the Indian telecom scenario. 'Anil was interested in knowing whether the business could still be profitable, since telecom rates had crashed in the recent past. And they were likely to go down further. I told him that lower rates would result in higher volumes, as had happened in the past two years with both number of subscribers and call times having jumped manifold,' explained Baijal.

In Mumbai's Reliance Centre, Anil's professional base, Amitabh was preparing the long-term strategy and vision paper for Infocomm. If Anil got Infocomm as part of the settlement process, he needed to be ready with a strategic blueprint. Earlier, he had said that everything was wrong about the company – its financing pattern, its strategy and business model. So, things had to change dramatically to make it a profitable and growing venture. The manner in which Mukesh approached the retail business, said his critics, was totally wrong, ill thought-out and unfriendly to customers.

The formal launch had been announced in December 2002 and, in retrospect, it was surprising that Anil did not attend the function. But the actual services were introduced through a soft launch two months later. The initial idea was simple or, as stated earlier, simplistic. Just force the phones down the customers' throats through the much-touted Dhirubhai Ambani Pioneer Scheme (DAPS). The idea: to get the world in your hands, literally.

Infocomm's direct-marketing juggernaut implied appointing 50,000 Dhirubhai Ambani Entrepreneurs (DAEs) across India to push its telecom services. The aim was to rope in 5 million customers – some say the target was only 2.5 million, although the company talked about 1 million subscribers every month – who would pay upfront charges of Rs 14,000 each. At 5 million, that would translate into Rs 7,000 crore immediate revenues. Since Infocomm, by that time, had invested Rs 9,000 crore in the telecom project, it would recoup most of its investments within months of the launch. However, Amitabh insisted that the actual figure that each subscriber had to pay upfront was Rs 22,000, which would have resulted in Infocomm getting more money than it had invested. This could be pumped back into the business, as the company needed to invest similar monies in the project over the next few years.

DAPS bombed. Infocomm managed only 1 million subscribers, and most of them were unwilling to pay money in advance. Instead, they were comfortable paying on a monthly basis. Cynics contended that the total number of customers was only half of what the company claimed. There were several reasons for this dismal failure. First was the choice of DAEs, as the company appointed anyone and everyone as its direct seller. Customers were wary of dealing with paanwallahs and neighbourhood grocers selling mobiles without any knowledge of either the technology or the scheme.

A business executive who was approached by one such DAE said that the agent had no idea about telecom, mobiles or the scheme. The only thing he could tell the potential buyer was that 'yeh bahut cheap hai' (this is a very cheap scheme). Other customers had similar experiences and realized that the scheme was being marketed unprofessionally – for instance, some DAEs had unreadable photocopies of the scheme. Even some of the DAEs found it difficult to get forms or relevant information from the company. A leading Mumbai-based broker, who promised 70,000 corporate connections, got only a quarter of the forms after a long wait.

Customers also realized that the Pioneer Scheme was not easy to comprehend. It had too many details in the fine print that no one read carefully in the initial stages. For instance, the handset was not coming in for free; the consumer was paying for it through a post-dated cheque. The promise of 'all calls at 40 paise per minute' was actually restricted to calls between two Reliance connections only. In a bid to get customers, the DAEs either glossed over such issues, or probably did not understand them. The result: scores of unhappy and unsatisfied customers.

In a candid and honest interview, Mukesh told a financial daily: 'There are a lot of things that don't work, and at the end of the day you should have the humility to say so, or nobody will try anything new.' Infocomm changed its marketing strategy – and shifted to the traditional retail-based selling. A company spokesperson told *Outlook*: 'Through customer feedback, we discovered the need for retail outlets where they can touch, feel and experience the handset. The critical need for a front-end was realized and we are now ready to provide consumers with a different retail experience.'

By the time Infocomm launched its 'Monsoon Hangama' scheme, it had learnt a few lessons. Customers queued up to become subscribers and Reliance Infocomm became the leading telecom services provider with over 10 million connections. But by that time, the company's business and financial model had gone for a six. It no longer had the satisfaction of getting money upfront. So more money had to be taken out of its cash cow, RIL, to finance expansion and setting up better infrastructure.

After these experiences, Anil thought that the entire marketing strategy had to be changed. Instead of chasing volumes – even if it was at a loss – Infocomm should chase upmarket customers – those who had the ability to pay and whose usage levels were very high – to boost its sagging bottomlines. That meant a radically different retail strategy. And it was Amitabh who was thinking about some of these changes. That too was a good enough indication that Infocomm was likely to go to Anil. Kamath's Option No. 1 was clearly the most acceptable to the two brothers.

Suddenly, however, in late April 2005, the Ambanis went to the public battlefield again to fight Round Two of the war. This time, the fight seemed more vicious than in the first round. Holidays were postponed, leaves were cancelled, and everyone was back to doing what they did best – street-fighting and sniping.

Initially, Anil was peeved by an unsigned note that sought to destroy the credibility of his Delhi-based advisor, Tony. I have disclosed its details in the first chapter; reference 'the note titled "The Spy As Executive".' Anil was furious at these below-the-belt tactics, and knew that the Mukesh camp was behind it. Another reason why things turned ugly was that the younger brother thought Mukesh's advisors were short-changing him in the deal – and that too behind his back.

The first inkling he got was in late April when his resignation from the two posts in IPCL – submitted in January 2005 – was quietly accepted. He only got to know while his advisors were browsing through IPCL's website and found that his name did not figure in the board of directors anymore. They were startled. Things – important ones – were happening without their knowledge. Till then, the IPCL had never admitted that it had accepted Anil's resignation from the two posts, which was submitted in January 2005. By doing so without his knowledge, IPCL – and Mukesh, who controlled it – was keeping Anil in the dark. Later, Mukesh's men said that Anil need not have got upset about it, because it was part of the deal that was currently being negotiated in a serious manner by the two brothers. Since IPCL was to come to Mukesh, there was no need for Anil to be represented on its board. In fact, IPCL had told the RoC about Anil's resignation on 28 March 2005.

Anil felt he should have been told. Besides, there were other transactions that were happening without his consent. After the IPCL board meeting in end-April, Anil came to know that Reliance Capital had sold IPCL shares in the open market, and that too at a massive loss. The official justification given by Mukesh's advisors was that the current market price was way below the acquisition price and, hence, Reliance Capital had to book a loss. It was a normal market transaction.

But it incensed Anil. For he felt there was no untoward reason to sell the shares at this critical juncture, when a deal was being finalized to split the group. Such a transfer, he told friends, should have happened only after the split agreement had been in place or a consensus had emerged on the valuations of the group's cross-holdings in different Ambani-owned companies. The sale went against his interests.

For if, as was expected, he got control of Reliance Capital, he would have insisted on a higher valuation for selling the IPCL shares to Mukesh and for getting out of the latter's management. The price of the IPCL shares would have been much higher than the market price. By selling these shares, the Mukesh camp had actually reduced his wealth while negotiations were going on. To this, the Mukesh camp insisted the sale was just a normal way to untangle the group's complex cross-holdings.

It was not as if only Anil was the aggrieved party. Even Mukesh was livid as he felt that his younger brother was deliberately delaying the settlement process. Anil was making fresh demands on Mukesh on almost a daily basis. First, Anil told Mukesh's negotiators that he desired a huge premium for his shares in RIL. For he was giving up management control and, therefore, had to be compensated on that front too. (If, as Kamath suggested, RIL went to Mukesh, the latter would have to buy out Anil's stake in the flagship.) This was no small change, and the difference that Anil was asking for would have resulted in a few thousand crore rupees extra in his kitty, depending on the exact valuation.

While Mukesh was ready to pay a small premium over the then existing RIL's scrip price of Rs 540, Anil was demanding Rs 750 per share. In its March 2004 report, Merrill Lynch had valued RIL's share at Rs 673 which, according to Anil, would have gone up due to improved operations and a slightly optimistic outlook for Reliance Infocomm. (In 2004-05, Infocomm posted a small net profit, after incurring a huge loss in the previous year.)

Mukesh agreed, but then countered by saying he too should be paid a premia for getting out of firms like Reliance Energy and Reliance Capital – which would go to Anil and in which RIL had substantial stakes. The elder brother also wanted a higher premia for his personal stake in Reliance Infocomm. Once again, while Anil thought the total value of the telecom venture was only Rs 20,000 crore, Mukesh felt the figure should be at least Rs 50,000 crore based on informal valuations by foreign analysts.

To put pressure on Anil, the elder brother put it in black and white that RIL would henceforth not lend any financial help to Reliance Infocomm. For Mukesh, this made sense as Anil had consistently criticized RIL's huge exposure to Infocomm. But now, Anil found it unacceptable, as he knew that telecom's future depended on help from the parent company. Infocomm needed Rs 5,000 crore in 2005-06 and Anil's estimates were that it would require a total of Rs 10,000-15,000 crore over the next few years.

Given this perspective, the talks had to break down some day. And they did towards the end of April. All the pent-up feelings came to the forefront the day RIL held its board meeting to announce the company's annual results for 2004-05. On 27 April 2005, Anil expressed his emotions in front of TV channels stationed outside Maker Chambers IV. That is when he gave his oft-quoted remark that this was a different sort of a cricket game, where he alone was playing against Mukesh XI. (Later, one of his advisors said that a better analogy would have been American football, where the touchdown expert is invariably tackled by several defenders at the same time.)

Anything to do with Reliance is laden with surprises. So, when everyone was gearing for a long-drawn-out battle like the previous one, there was a lull again. In the first week of May, Amitabh said that Nikhil Meswani, the cousin of the two brothers who was now briefing journalists from Mukesh's side, had no locus standi to speak on family-related matters. Since Nikhil wasn't involved in the division process, he wouldn't – and couldn't – know the nitty gritties of the discussion and, therefore, should clam up.

I found it ironical. In January 2005, both Amitabh and Tony were briefing journalists about the so-called – but non-existent – deal that had been accepted by both the Ambani brothers. So while Anil had no qualms about his advisors talking on family-related issues, he had a problem if his cousin did so. Anyway, Anil's ploy worked perfectly. Nikhil did clam up and the other advisors too went into a shell. 'We want to play by the rules,' said one of them. Another one refused to take any calls. The third referred me to Nikhil who,

I was told, had stopped all briefings. Anil's advisors too followed suit.

The lull meant that the two sides were back at the negotiating table. This time, hopefully, they would not get up till they clicked a deal.

The hopes were not belied. It was not long before the Ambanis were smoking the peace pipe.

7
Dhirubhai's Legacy

Thus it is that in war the victorious strategist only seeks battle after the victory has been won, whereas he who is destined to defeat first fights and afterwards looks for victory.

— The Art of War by Sun Tzu

First establish your near-monopolistic place in hitherto unknown territories, and then force others to fall in line.

— Ambani interpretation

The late Dhirubhai was not just one person. He was several characters at different points of time in his life – and showed different shades of his myriad personality at any given moment. Thus it's difficult to straitjacket one of India's most high-profile businessmen who was variously esoteric, flamboyant, ambitious, visionary, mercenary, aggressive, a street-fighter and manipulator par excellence.

It is virtually impossible to write a definitive biography of his, or even a substantive history of Reliance and the House of Ambanis. For people who met Dhirubhai at different times would remember him differently. He was a man on the move, a man with only his goals – both long-term and short-term – on his mind. He was Arjuna who, at any given point, saw only the fish's eye. He was Krishna, who had no scruples when it came to battle — the end justified the means.

Therefore, Dhirubhai would change paths, go off an a tangent, take several U-turns – do anything that would take him closer to his overriding objective of making Reliance India's, and later the world's, biggest corporate group. Dhirubhai was in a great rush to do in two decades what others had achieved in twice or thrice that period. He was, as Albert Einstein might have put it, a four-dimensional man – you had to look at all the four space and time coordinates to understand and comprehend his actions.

Dhirubhai would remain a mystery to most, a myth to many, and sinister to a few. He was God, Demi-God and Satan – all in one lifetime. By the time of his death in July 2002, he was revered, respected, hated, loathed, but never ignored. He had become an institution in himself, so big that no one could touch him. But that was not the way it always was.

Probably the best way to describe the man and his legacy is to look at his actions and decisions during critical phases of his life and career. For a sequential account of his life will not capture his essence or his character. Before that, however, a short biographical sketch is in order. He was born in Chorwad (literal translation: settlement of thieves) in Saurashtra (Gujarat). His father was a failed trader who then taught in a local primary school. Being born in a Gujarati trader family, Dhirubhai went to the British protectorate of Aden to try his luck in business, like so many others of his clan,. Officially, he worked at A. Besse & Co, one of the largest and most powerful trading houses that dealt in a wide range of products in the Arab world and Africa. It was in Aden that his trading, risk-taking and astute decision-making talent came to the fore.

Hamish McDonald's *The Polyester Prince* brings out this aspect in graphical detail. In the early 1950s, wrote McDonald, Yemenese officials noticed a shortage in their country's currency, rial, which was a solid silver coin. Inquiries led them to an unknown Indian clerk, Dhirubhai, based in Aden, who was openly buying all rials from the local market. This shrewd Gujarati had realized that the market value of the silver content in the coin was higher than the rial's exchange value.

Dhirubhai was simply buying rials, melting the coins and selling the silver at a small profit. Despite wafer-thin margins, he told McDonald that he made a few lakhs of rupees in the three months before Yemen put a stop to the practice. Ambani loyalists are full of such Aden stories, where Dhirubhai took several risks playing the commodities market, especially rice and sugar. He learnt, he went nearly bankrupt a few times, he was helped by friends and relatives, and he also made some money.

By the time he returned to India in 1958 with his wife Kokilaben and son Mukesh – the other three children, Anil, Dipti and Nina were born in India – Dhirubhai was ready to make his name in the textile mart.

In the synthetic yarn sector, shortages were rampant due to small local capacities. And these were made up either by smuggling or imports through what were called replenishment (REP) licences. These licences were issued by the government to actual users, who could import synthetic yarn without paying any customs duties to churn out cloth in their factories, and they could not be transferred to anyone else. But the REP licences were openly sold at a premium to anyone who was interested. Policy makers either did not know about it or did not care as long as they issued a specific number of licences entitling the holders to import specific quantities only.

Soon Dhirubhai realized he could make a killing on the streets of Pydhonie (literal translation: foot bath, and legend has it that there was one there in the olden days), the textile trading centre in central Mumbai's Girgaon area. If he could buy enough of these licences at whatever premia, he could still make profits, as polyester yarn prices in India were much higher than those prevailing in the global market. He soon became a major player in the REP licences business. Taking their cue from Dhirubhai, a number of other Indian entrepreneurs like Abhey Oswal (the breakaway faction of the Ludhiana-based Oswal group) and the Vachanis of the Delhi-based Weston group used REP licences in the 1980s and early 1990s to import products that were in short supply in India, and sold them at good profit margins. Weston did so with electronics items and Oswal with several products.

The trader (that Dhirubhai was) turned into a part-manufacturer by installing a few knitting machines in the mid-1960s. While he kept expanding the manufacturing infrastructure – within thirteen years, the factory area had increased twenty-three times and had machines for several processes like crimping, twisting and weaving synthetic yarns – it was his perceptiveness as a trader that generated higher profits. From REP licences, he moved on to a more lucrative higher unit value scheme initiated by the government in the early 1970s.

Earlier, under the REP scheme, exporters of nylon fabrics could only get nylon fibre (a raw material) into the country. However, under the new scheme, they could even import duty-free polyester yarn against nylon fibre exports. But there was a catch: exporters now had to sell nylon fabrics at a price that was double of what the government earlier stipulated under REP licences. Thus, Dhirubhai was forced to seek export markets for nylon to be able to import polyester. He used the Gujarati network abroad – those he had met in Aden or close relatives and friends – to find global buyers. The calculations were simple: if he could find enough buyers, he could sell the imported polyester yarn at seven to eight times the international price.

As was normally the case with REP licences, traders misused the new scheme also. The trick was to over-invoice nylon fabrics exports, that is, show a higher price, to become entitled to higher value of import licences. The difference between the actual export price and the higher one stated in the invoice would be paid to the buyer through the havala route, that is, sending out black money made in India to any global destination by paying a premium. This would be more than made up through profits on imported polyester yarn, as the difference between the domestic and international price was seven to eight times in those days.

Dhirubhai and his loyalists always claimed he never did anything illegal. What Dhirubhai was good at was interpreting the law and finding loopholes that could earn profits from him. He did the same with REP licences and the higher unit value scheme. In both cases Dhirubhai asserted that he did the legitimate thing – buy REP licences or export nylon fabrics by putting pressure on his managers to find new markets to get import entitlements. Both were perfectly legal and within the boundaries of the law.

Much later, in the 1990s, it seemed ironical that the man who made his initial money through the lucrative imports business found himself on the wrong side of the trading business. By that time, Dhirubhai had established Reliance as a renowned manufacturer and had got out of trading totally. The 1992-97 export-import (Exim) policy announced by the then commerce minister, P. Chidambaram, allowed duty-free imports of any product (whether it was needed as an input or not) against exports. The imports could be effected even before the exports had commenced. The only restrictions under the new value-based advance licensing (Vabal) scheme was that the value of imports should be the same as the cif (cost-insurance-freight) value of exports, and the products included in a separate sensitive list could not be imported.

The new provision opened up a Pandora's box. Suddenly, exporters had a choice to import items that were in shortage in the domestic market and, therefore, commanded huge premia. One of those several products happened to be plastic, which Reliance started manufacturing in 1991 when the phase one of its Hazira cracker complex was commissioned. A fear psychosis gripped Dhirubhai and he feared that the huge investments sunk in this segment could go down a plastic tube.

Within no time, the Reliance investigators were pushed into action. Their job: to find out names of exporters who had got Vabal licences, to what extent, against what exports, and whether they were legitimate exporters or not. The final result: hundreds of pages of documents that allegedly proved that there was a huge scam in the Vabal scheme.

Working through their own networks, and operating through a credible front – an organization called the Chemicals & Petrochemicals Manufacturers Association (CPMA) – Reliance convinced people that Vabal licences were issued to import plastic against fictitious exports. Exporters were showing export invoices, not actually exporting any goods, bringing in foreign exchange in lieu of sales through the havala route, getting advance licences to import huge quantities of plastic, selling either plastic or the licences locally at huge premia because of yawning differential between international and domestic prices of plastic, and laughing all the way to the bank. (Remember what had happened in the case of REP and high unit value licences!)

Let me quote from a bulky investigative report that was submitted by the CPMA in February 1994 to the directorate general of foreign trade, which was under the commerce ministry and regulated international trade. The report claimed that some of the firms with licences were fictitious. In addition, it alleged that many firms had got licences to import huge quantities of plastic which were way above their entitlements or requirements. Most of the licencees were small and medium-size garment exporters, whose only need for plastics was for packaging – and that couldn't be more than 10 per cent of their turnover. But they were sitting on licences that entitled them to import plastics worth crores of rupees each. Going by the industry norms, the CPMA charged that these firms were 'misusing' Vabal and had to be exporting between Rs 50-100 crore each of readymade garments to be able to use those quantities of plastics as packaging material.

While the debate was raging among users, manufacturers, traders and government officials, Chidambaram, who, by then had resigned his portfolio due to his alleged involvement in the 1992 Harshad Mehta scam, told his friends that people were making a mountain out of a molehill. The whole purpose of the Vabal scheme, he said, was to boost export earnings and reduce India's trade deficit. Whether the exports were genuine or not did not matter as long as the foreign exchange actually flowed in. As long as exporters remitted, or brought back, the money, it was good for the economy.

Finally, however, Reliance won at the end of day. Plastic products were initially put in the sensitive list, rules governing Vabal were consistently tightened, the scheme went through several changes and imports affecting the Ambanis came to a grinding halt. Much later, the Comptroller and Auditor General concluded that Vabal was misused to a large extent. Yet again, Dhirubhai had made everyone realize he could play any game and win hands down. As he had done and proved so many times in the past few decades.

It was in the 1980s that Dhirubhai graduated from a risk-taking and calculating trader to an ambitious, visionary, yet cut-throat, manufacturer. The game was different, the rules had changed, but the trader showed he had several aces up his sleeve — more than the usual four in a pack.

Dhirubhai's gameplan included two new aspects — woo investors and grow big. The first was the most critical and it made the Ambanis a household name across the country. Later, the family became an idol for scores of global institutions too. Like it or not, Dhirubhai can safely be credited with the tag of one who unleashed the stock market forces in India and virtually created 'an equity cult' with millions of investors as members.

In October 1977, RIL (then Reliance Textiles Industries) went public by giving out nearly 3 million shares at face value (of Rs 10 per share) to outside investors. That was just the beginning of an equity blitzkrieg. By the mid-1980s, the company had raised Rs 940 crore through the markets. In the process, it changed all the rules of investing; in some cases, it pressurized and cajoled policy makers to do that. That enabled Dhirubhai to raise enormous cash, which was essential to finance RIL's ambitious forays into making polyester yarn and its key petrochemical intermediates.

One of his brilliant moves was the use of convertible debentures, which is paper issued by a company that earned a specified rate of interest initially but was later converted into equity shares, usually at a high premium. It allowed investors to earn decent returns until the company had commissioned its new plant, and then they could earn even higher returns due to market appreciation of the price of their shares. The company gained by earning huge premia by converting debentures into shares at an appropriate time and, therefore, boosting its balance sheet and managing to keep its equity base low. The magical Dhirubhai even managed the impossible – getting government permission to convert non-convertible debentures into shares. Obviously, there was a frenzy to buy any paper related to RIL – shares, convertible debentures, non-convertible debentures – due to the expectations that everything would finally be converted into shares, whose market price could only skyrocket to ever-higher levels.

Investors lined up to buy RIL stock, and Dhirubhai could boast of over a million investors by 1986. (Today, the figure for Reliance group companies is 3.5 million.) In December 1986, while advertising for one of its debenture issues, RIL claimed that Rs 1000 invested in its shares in 1977 would have led to a total return of Rs 1,10,041 in November 1986, or an appreciation of just under 11,000 per cent. Other studies showed lower appreciation figures, but were still mind boggling.

Hamish McDonald said that 'an analysis by S.R. Mohnot... points out that to obtain the value quoted (by RIL) in 1986, the investor would have had to top up his initial Rs 1000 outlay by subscribing to every rights issue (offered to shareholders in a certain ratio) and debenture issue (a portion could be set aside for shareholders) offered to him, taking the total investment to nearly Rs 30,000 for assets and accumulated earnings (interest and dividends) worth Rs 1,08,278. This was far from thousands of percentage points but still equivalent to an annual compound rate of interest of 44.5 per cent. Tellingly, Mohnot noted that, had the investor bailed out at the end of 1983 after five years, the annual compounded return would have been a still more impressive 75 per cent.'

Even in those early days, Dhirubhai's increasing influence over investors was not without a few crises. The biggest one came in March 1982, when a known cartel of bear operators – the market jargon for sellers of stocks – started hammering down the scrips of several companies, including RIL, through a wave of selling pressure on the Bombay Stock Exchange (BSE). Dhirubhai couldn't take it lying down. For declining share price could upset all his manufacturing calculations. He had to strike back.

Out of nowhere, a set of brokers emerged who purchased every single share that was available in the market to prop up the declining share price. They were buying the shares on behalf of a few NRIs based in west Asian countries too. Now, the bluff started between the bulls – market jargon for buyers – and the bears. Who would blink first? Who would show their cards first? Who would force the other down on their knees?

The Indian bourses in those days were immature. The settlements, that is, reconciliation of all daily transactions (sales and purchases) were done on a fortnightly basis on every second Friday. But essentially, the settlements were driven by the buyers, who had the right to demand deliveries or accept badla or an interest of sorts to allow sellers to carry their positions over to the next fortnightly settlement period. For nearly six weeks or so, the buyers of RIL stock allowed the sellers to carry forward their positions. And then came the body blow.

On 30 April 1986, the buyers demanded deliveries of all the shares that had been sold. A right that they had under the settlement system. The bears were caught in a jam. They had sold shares on the expectation that the RIL scrip price would crash and that they would make a huge profit by squaring off their positions. Suddenly, they were scrambling for the shares to deliver to the buyers. It led to a major crisis and there were apprehensions that the bears could default. The RIL scrip soared and crossed the Rs 200 mark in anticipation that the buyers were in a position to squeeze the sellers dry. Things were sorted out by 10 May 1986 when the bears either found some way to deliver the shares or paid the difference between the price at which they had sold the shares and the then prevailing market price (which was much higher) to reconcile – or 'square off', as they say it in market parlance – their 'sell' positions. By then, as RIL scrip price skyrocketed, the bulls or buyers had won the battle, and Dhirubhai emerged as the messiah of investors and the king of BSE.

That it was Dhirubhai's hand behind the bulls started becoming clear in 1983, when the then finance minister, Pranab Mukherjee, doled out details in Parliament on NRI investments in the Indian bourses. In his budget in February 1982, Mukherjee had allowed NRIs to invest in Indian stocks on a repatriable basis, which meant the non-resident buyers could take their money out after selling the shares. Earlier, they were forced to keep the proceeds of the sale in India. The RBI implemented the new policy in April 1982, just when Dhirubhai was getting ready to launch his counter-attack against the bears.

It seemed an uncanny coincidence, and there's no evidence to link the two events. Probably, the stars, as usual, were on Dhirubhai's side. But on 10 May 1983, Mukherjee revealed that between April 1982 and April 1983, eleven NRIs had bought shares worth Rs 22.50 crore in two Indian firms. No one attached much importance to it as it was assumed that the two firms were Escorts and DCM, and that the overseas Indians must be connected to the UK-based NRI-businessman, Swraj Paul, who had recently launched takeover raids on the former firms.

Within a week, *Business Standard* found out that the NRIs had invested majorly in RIL and, as Mukherjee confirmed later in July, that 98 per cent of the NRI inflows had been used to buy RIL. The finance minister was forced to give further details when the Reliance connection came out. He said the eleven firms operated out of the UK and revealed their names. A couple of them had comical ones – Crocodile Investments and Fiasco Investments. Some of these tantalizing clues were picked up by *The Telegraph*, which was then owned by the same management as *Business Standard*.

Months later, *The Telegraph's* investigations revealed that none of the eleven firms were registered in the UK. In eight of the cases, the registry applications were moved on 27 July 1983, a day after FM Mukherjee gave additional details on the eleven firms in Parliament. In November 1983, the finance minister tabled a correction – the eleven firms were actually registered in Isle of Man, a known tax haven for global investors. In the following months, other publications embarked on their own investigations in a bid to lift the veil off the firms that had their bases in a tax haven.

India Today was one of the few that managed to dig out fascinating details. It found that most of the companies, which had been registered between 1979 and 1982, had Krishna Shah of Leicester and his family members as directors. Other Indian names that figured as directors were the three members of the Dhamani family and a couple, Praful and Nalini Shah from New York. Now hear what happened as it appears in McDonald's *The Polyester Prince*: 'A mystified *India Today* reported that Krishna Shah was a former Leicester city councillor, born in Kenya, who had come to Britain in 1959 and initially worked as a train guard with British Rail, before opening his own shop and then setting up a small knitwear factory which employed five people only. Shah told the magazine's reporter he knew nothing about any companies in the Isle of Man.

'Someone in the (eleven) companies was remarkably well informed on investment conditions in India, however. On 20 August 1982, the RBI lifted a Rs 100,000 ceiling on share investments in any one company by non-resident Indians. Three days later, three of the Isle of Man companies applied to the (Indian) central bank to invest Rs 20 million each in Reliance. Four other companies applied together on 24 September. Six companies made their purchases on the same day, 15 October, at the same share price, which was a significant discount to the then market price.

'While each company had a paid-up capital of only 200 pounds, three of them had managed to talk the European Asian Bank to lend identical amounts of $1.65 million to each, through the bank's branch in Colombo, Sri Lanka, on 26 October 1982. All three bought Reliance shares at the same price, Rs 128 (per share). It was a sound piece of investigation, but no link with Dhirubhai had been found and many questions remained unanswered.' Finally, McDonald claims to have found the 'smoking gun' evidence.

'Had the reporters spread their questions wider in the Gujarati diaspora, they might have discovered a very odd connection. The leading name in Crocodile, Fiasco, et al, was the same Krishna Kant Shah and fellow student activist whom Dhirubhai helped spring from jail after the 1947 communal riot in Junagadh,' he wrote.

While in school (Bahadur Kunj School in Junagadh), Dhirubhai got involved with India's freedom movement struggle. He became a leading star in Junagadh Vidyarthi Sangh, which did the usual things, like organizing meetings to salute the then Congress flag and hold motivation sessions to mark their opposition to British rule. Post-Independence on 15 August 1947, Junagadh erupted because its ruler announced its accession to Pakistan. This created a problem because Junagadh was a landlocked area surrounded by Hindu-ruled states that had decided to join India.

Junagadh was rocked by communal violence between Hindus and Muslims. During one of these riots, which were finally stemmed when the Indian army entered the state in November 1947 and took control, the students of the Junagadh Vidyarthi Sangh went to an affected area to protect shops owned by Muslims. The police misunderstood and arrested Krishna Kant Shah, who was a boarding house companion of Dhirubhai. And it was Dhirubhai who talked to police officials and managed to get Shah out within hours. This, says McDonald, was the same Krishna Kant Shah of Leicester, who was a director in many of the eleven firms in the Isle of Man. Let's turn back to McDonald's book.

'After finishing his education, Shah had gone back to join the family business in Kenya. In 1964, he moved to Britain on his own, working for an engineering company for two years and then as a railway guard for eight years. In 1970, he quit British Rail and set up his own shop in Leicester's Hartingdon Road, selling hardware, saris, utensils and religious statues, and living in a flat upstairs. (One can see a number of discrepancies between the years – *India Today* said Shah came to Britain in

1959, and McDonald thinks it was 1964. But if the latter year is correct, Shah couldn't have worked for two years for a company and eight years for British Rail and still open his shop in 1970.)

'His customer base was the fellow Gujaratis then congregating in Leicester after their expulsion from Uganda by Idi Amin at forty-eight hours notice in 1972, and the more gradual squeeze out of Kenya by Jomo Kenyatta's "Africanization" of commerce. By the mid-1990s, about one-quarter of the city's 400,000 population were immigrants, about 80,000 of them South Asian. Almost all the 65,000 Hindus were Gujaratis...

'Clearly, Shah did not have millions of dollars to put into Reliance shares, or the financial knowledge to set up elaborate ownership arrangements through the Isle of Man, where he had never been, or to take out loans from a foreign bank in Sri Lanka to finance the purchase of shares in India through an Isle of Man company.

'He had, however, kept in touch with Dhirubhai, and his wife Induben had become a good friend of Dhirubhai's wife Kokilaben. On trips to buy textile machinery in Britain, Dhirubhai would take Shah along, while Shah introduced Reliance's export manager Rathibhai Muchhala to many of the South Asian retailers in Leicester. In 1972, Dhirubhai brought his wife and children to Britain for a holiday and the two families spent some time together. Later that year Shah's oldest son Sailash, who had just completed a diploma in textile manufacturing, went off to a job at the Reliance factory in Naroda, where he stayed five years before returning to Leicester to help his father set up the new knitwear business. In 1977, Dhirubhai provided two cars for Sailash's wedding.

'Krishna Kant Shah died in 1986 in the midst of a fresh controversy about the mysterious Isle of Man companies. At a meeting in 1995, Sailash Shah maintained there had been no business connection between his father and Dhirubhai. Asked how it was that the Indian press and investigators had singled out his family as Dhirubhai's fronts, he would say only: "I don't know how."' But the Isle of Man issue, the confrontation with the dreaded bear cartel, and the numerous innovations Reliance offered to stock investors, made Dhirubhai a darling among Indian investors. From the 1980s, and even till today, Reliance is the most fancied stock despite the volatile ups and downs in RIL's scrip.'

To grow rapidly as an entrepreneur and make the transition into a renowned manufacturer, Dhirubhai's second strategy was to think big. As in the past, he used his influence and growing network of friends and loyalists to manage policy makers. In the early 1980s, he got the licence to manufacture polyester yarn. The surprising thing about it was that Reliance was one of only three companies – of the over forty firms that applied – which got a licence. And that too for 10,000 tonnes per annum capacity, compared to 6,000 tonnes for the other two. Obviously, Reliance was on its way to bigger things. Its eyes were also set on setting up a huge plant to make PTA, or pure terephthallic acid, a key ingredient to make polyester and a substitute for DMT (di-methyl terephthalate) that was being made by Bombay Dyeing by 1985. (Reliance got a preliminary clearance to make 75,000 tonnes per annum of PTA in late 1984 and it commenced commercial production in May 1988.)

By this time a vicious, vitriolic war between Reliance and Bombay Dyeing was brewing in the air. It was going to be one of the fiercest battles in Indian corporate history. It was a fight to decide the superiority of two petrochemicals, which are known better for their acronyms – PTA and DMT. It was a battle that involved politics, media, egos, economics – in fact, everything including the technical and incomprehensible debate on which is a better input to manufacture polyester. It also established Dhirubhai as a successful street fighter – one who knew how to influence powerful quarters to stymie systematic attacks on his empire by his competitors.

It's difficult to hazard a guess as to why Dhirubhai and Nusli Wadia, the high profile and suave Parsi who owned Bombay Dyeing, hated each other. There are too many theories floated by one camp or the other. Looked at from a purely business perspective, it was probably Wadia's feeling that Reliance was responsible for delays in Bombay Dyeing getting the requisite permissions to import a second-hand plant to make DMT and the Ambanis' smear campaign to prove that Wadia's plant was 'junk' and that DMT was a much inferior product compared to PTA. Reliance was already using PTA as an intermediate to make polyester yarn.

Going by the size of the polyester market in 1985-86, it was obvious that only one player – either Bombay Dyeing or Reliance – would survive. If the industry – and the government – accepted DMT was a better product, the pendulum would swing towards Wadia. If not, Dhirubhai would become the polyester king. It was a fight to decide who would call the shots – and who would control the sector for decades to come.

One of the numerous anonymous notes issued by Reliance corporate communications division against DMT was in the mid-1980s, when Bombay Dyeing had commenced local production of DMT and Reliance was only an importer of PTA although it was planning to set up a domestic unit to manufacture the polyester intermediate. The contents of the note provide a hint as to why Wadia would have been furious with Dhirubhai. 'The conventional method of producing PSF/PFY (polyester staple fibre and polyester filament yarn) was by using DMT as the raw material. PTA is the latest innovation in the international market. As against DMT, PTA is economical and does not give a by-product, methanol. Most of the plants in the international field are using PTA as the raw material... As per the consumers of DMT in the country, while the quality of IPCL and Bongaigon (which were two of three manufacturers, apart from Bombay Dyeing) is acceptable, Bombay Dyeing's quality of DMT is considered sub-standard. These two (DMT and PTA) are not interchangeable (and cannot be used by the users of one or the other), as claimed by some vested interests... It is interesting to note that except one application approved by the government since enunciation of the import policy in 1985, no application from any other applicant has been considered for issuance of licence for import of DMT.' The message was loud and clear.

The Congress government, led by the late Rajiv Gandhi, had increased the import duties on PTA and DMT. It was a move that could harm Reliance, a PTA importer, and benefit Bombay Dyeing, a DMT producer which now had the luxury to keep its domestic selling price slightly above the landed cost of imported DMT. Wadia, whose future depended on DMT and who thought he was more powerful at that time, decided it was time to retaliate against Dhirubhai with all the forces at his command. For, despite being in a stronger position, he could not afford Reliance's smear campaign against DMT to succeed. He also could not let Reliance set up its huge PTA unit and compete with Bombay Dyeing.

Somehow Wadia joined hands with newspaper baron, Ramnath Goenka, whose *Indian Express* went all out to sink the Reliance ship. It nearly succeeded as Dhirubhai suffered a paralytic stroke in 1986. But then, like many others, they had underestimated the might of the Ambanis. In the end, despite the attacks, Dhirubhai raced much ahead of Bombay Dyeing – today the Reliance group is several times larger than Wadia's. PTA won the war against DMT – most polyester users use PTA – and it was Dhirubhai who became India's Polyester Prince. But it didn't always look that way; especially when the first attacks on Reliance began in the mid-1980s.

Among the several pieces that S. Gurumurthy, who spearheaded the *Express* campaign, wrote against Reliance was on the latter's import of two plants – one to make polyester yarn and the other to produce PTA. In both cases, the allegations were similar: that Reliance had imported plant and machinery that were capable of producing nearly twice as much quantity as had been specified on their licences. As Gurumurthy repeatedly reiterated: Reliance had smuggled in an additional plant without the knowledge of either the customs department or other government agencies. The allegation was effective as the customs department later issued two separate show cause notices to Reliance on the import of the two units.

In 1988-89, Parliament's Public Accounts Committee, headed by Amal Datta, had this to say about the import of RIL's polyester yarn unit. 'This report of the Committee deals with a case of unauthorized importations of plant and machinery, misdeclaration and under-invoicing of goods involving customs duty of Rs 119.64 crore by a textiles manufacturer (Reliance Industries Ltd) for their project at Patalganga in Maharashtra for the manufacture of polyester filament yarn, as alleged in a show cause notice issued by the customs department on 10 February, 1987...

'The Committee has noted with concern that the customs authorities were blissfully unaware of the alleged import of four additional machines. They have recommended that the Ministry of Finance should take adequate steps to streamline the procedure and make customs control more effective in respect of goods imported under project contract right from the stage of their import till the stage of final assessment of customs duty thereon.

'The Committee has expressed their surprise that even though the show cause notice was issued on 10 February 1987, the Enforcement Directorate are yet to form their view on the possible FERA (Foreign Exchange Regulations Act) violation in this case. They have been of the firm view that irrespective of the fact whether the case involved violations or otherwise, the reluctance on the part of Enforcement Directorate to act with the required firmness is questionable and highly deplorable. The Committee has recommended that the Enforcement Directorate should act with a better degree of firmness and promptitude to check economic offences of the alleged nature.'

Once the customs department checked the Patalganga unit, the Committee stated that the former found several discrepancies. 'Based on the study of the agreement with the supplier/technical collaborators and production noticed during inspection, the customs officers team estimated the capacity of the plant to be over 55,000 metric tonnes per annum. According to them, this was more than double the licensed capacity. The re-endorsement of the industrial licence (issued to RIL by the government) was for 25,125 metric tonnes per annum in November 1984. They concluded that as per import licences, the importer was allowed to import eight spinning machines only in the initial setting up and substantial expansion, while twelve machines were found to be installed.'

Much later, on 11 May 1990, the customs department issued another show cause notice on RIL. This time, the allegation was that the company had imported a PTA-manufacturing plant that was capable of producing at least twice the quantity than was sanctioned to it by the government (75,000 tonnes per annum). Logically, there were allegations of smuggling an additional plant.

In response, Dhirubhai came out with guns blazing in all directions. He contested the show cause notices legally. He rallied support from friends in the media, bureaucracy and among politicians. He attacked Wadia, as he thought the Parsi entrepreneur was engineering the show cause notices to RIL. And Dhirubhai won when the government did not take any major action against RIL on the above charges. The files pertaining to these cases sat on a desk and kept collecting dust. It seemed that Reliance had somehow succeeded in its salvage and defence operations.

Still, the Ambani-Wadia fight – which panned out for over a decade and one can still witness a few skirmishes here and there – turned out to be one until death. It was a fight where the end definitely justified the means. The Wadia-Goenka-Gurumurthy combine left no stone unturned to destroy Dhirubhai. The trio vigorously hurled new salvos at Reliance – be it the company's new issue to raise funds, an application to expand or diversify, or a policy change that seemed to favour Reliance. It turned out to be a classic street battle. And it generated a series of below-the-belt blows from both sides to discredit the other. The worst of these exchanges happened in the 1990s.

For Wadia, it was a scathing assault on his character. Dhirubhai was gleeful when one of Wadia's enemies – the late Rajan Pillai and then owner of the Britannia group – alleged that the Bombay Dyeing chief had a second British passport that he was still using in the early 1990s. Then, about seventy MPs wrote a letter stating the same and added more charges against Wadia. They said Wadia was involved in destabilizing the country's government in 1987, when Rajiv Gandhi was in power. He was close to foreign intelligence agencies, including Pakistan's ISI (Inter State Intelligence). Even Wadia's antecedents as the grandson of Jinnah were used to hint that his actions were anti-national.

Wadia had no option but to call a press conference on 19 August 1993 to clear his name. Here's a summary of his statement, which indicated the level to which the two corporate rivals had stooped in a bid to destroy each other.

'The letter of the MPs mentions... he (Mr Wadia) hired an ex-CIA operative... to defame and destabilize the government of Shri Rajiv Gandhi... (and it) was duly examined and proved by a commission of inquiry... This is not at all true. No charge was proved. The letter alleges that I have been charged with the unauthorized and criminal use of an undisclosed (British) passport. This is a false allegation. A copy of my letter to the (Indian) home minister along with proof of my British passports having been cancelled on 7th November 1990 at the time when I got Indian citizenship and Indian passport is attached... The letter alleges that I have been charged in 1993 of having forged Indian diplomatic passport. This is totally false. I have never possessed or used an Indian diplomatic passport at any time.'

He also dismissed allegations that he was in touch with the ISI, that Indian intelligence wings had evidence against him, that he instigated Harshad Mehta, who was implicated in the 1992 stock market scam, to say that the latter paid money to the then prime minister Narasimha Rao, that he travelled to several countries on his British passport, that he had secret business and financial interests in Singapore, Switzerland, Paris, US, British Virgin Islands, Pakistan, Dubai and Nepal, that he had visited Dubai before the Bombay blasts in 1992 and met underworld leaders, and that he owed the Indian exchequer over Rs 60 crore as dues and penalties for non-payment of personal income and wealth tax.

On the flip side, the Ambanis were under a cloud over their proposed takeover of L&T (then Larsen & Toubro). The trio of Wadia-Goenka-Gurumurthy projected it as a covert attempt to annex a professionally managed company. When the trio exposed the role of a few financial institutions in allegedly helping Reliance and sought legal remedies, the government was forced to intervene and stall the ambitions of the Ambanis. Finally, Reliance let go of L&T and Dhirubhai gave up the company's chairmanship.

The 1980s and the early part of the 1990s were a period of high drama, tumult and excitement, which also exposed the thin fabric of India's democracy. In those two decades, every political move or economic decision was somehow linked to Ambani or Wadia. If one had to believe these rumours, they brought down governments, governments came to power because of their backing, politicians took sides openly, and policies were clearly tuned to help one or the other. Obviously, only some of it was true. But it was a time when there was only one truth – that the war between Dhirubhai and Nusli would engulf anyone and everyone.

It nearly did. It probably played a part in bringing down two governments – that of Rajiv Gandhi in 1989 as the Congress lost in the national elections due to several controversies that indirectly had their origins in the Dhirubhai-Wadia battle; and that of V.P. Singh in 1991. The lives of Rajiv Gandhi, V.P. Singh, Dhirubhai Ambani and Nusli Wadia were interlinked in dramatic fashion in the years between 1984 and 1991. In 1984, when Rajiv assumed power after the death of his mother Indira Gandhi – who was assassinated by her bodyguards – he decided to demolish the growing nexus between politicians and corporates in India. In a bid to don this clean image, he selected V.P. Singh, known as an honest politician, as his finance minister. Singh launched a carrot-and-stick policy against Indian business groups he thought were at the root of the problem. Among others, his main target was also the Reliance group. He raided several companies, arrested big corporate owners, and launched investigations against their wrongdoings. Dhirubhai found himself surrounded by powerful enemies – the FM himself, Bhure Lal – Singh's friend and the head of the Enforcement Directorate who started revisiting all the past Reliance cases, and the Wadia-Goenka-Gurumurthy trio that seemed capable of influencing the government.

At the height of the onslaught against Reliance, the situation changed when two letters – now proven forged – reached Rajiv Gandhi. They stated that the government of India, rather the finance ministry and Bhure Lal, had hired the services of a US-based detective agency, Fairfax, to investigate the activities of Ajitabh Bachchan, an NRI based in Britain. Rajiv was furious – after all, Ajitabh was the brother of one of his closest family friends, the film star-politician-businessman Amitabh Bachchan. The letters also stated that Wadia, Gurumurthy and Goenka were in touch with Fairfax's promoter, Michael Hershman, and other employees of the detective agency.

The letters created an irreparable wedge between Rajiv and V.P. Singh. Bhure Lal, who was caught in the rift, was shunted out. The Congress government launched investigations against the trio – Gurumurthy was questioned, Goenka's *Indian Express* was raided and Wadia found himself totally out of favour with the regime. The situation became more complicated when the *Indian Express* revealed the contents of a letter, written by the then president of India, Giani Zail Singh, which criticized Rajiv and his government. The rumour in the political circles was that Giani Zail Singh wanted to dismiss the Rajiv Gandhi government. Finally, when the dust settled on this affair, the FM too had been relieved of his portfolio, and Dhirubhai was apparently close to the Congress circles. The tide had shifted in Reliance's favour. Almost all the cases pending against the group were put in cold storage. But the Fairfax and the Giani Zail Singh affairs ruptured the Congress party as it forced politicians to choose between Rajiv or V.P. Singh, Reliance or Bombay Dyeing. More important, it started a sequence of events that finally led to allegations against the Rajiv Gandhi regime that its senior politicians had been paid bribes in at least two defence deals – Bofors and HDW. In the 1989 elections, the Congress lost, largely due to the still unproven allegation that Rajiv had personally taken money in the Bofors deal. What one heard in hushed whispers in those days was that the forged letters were the handiwork of an interested corporate!

In 1989, when V.P. Singh became the prime minister, as the head of a National Front government, Dhirubhai found himself with his back against the wall – once again. All the cases against Reliance were revived. Fresh action was initiated, Singh played a major role in stalling and derailing Reliance's attempts to take over L&T (mentioned earlier). Within months, however, fissures were created in the National Front government, Singh found himself fighting several political battles at the same time, he just did not seem to have the political backing to prosecute Dhirubhai or Reliance. Finally, Singh's government fell. Yet again, the whispers were the same – the shadow of a corporate loomed behind Singh's political downfall.

But by the mid-1990s, Dhirubhai was on a different path. The country saw yet another of his facets, when he pushed his group on to the global arena. Events that led to this new transformation were put into action much earlier, but their culmination happened then. In this endeavour, his two sons, Mukesh and Anil, who had joined the business in the 1980s and watched everything as active participants, adequately helped Dhirubhai. The successful commissioning of the Hazira petrochemicals cracker and the Jamnagar refinery put the Reliance group in a different league. Without any apparent warning, the House of Ambanis became so huge that its competitors and enemies were left way behind. In comparison, Wadia seemed puny and weak. Size matters, and in the case of the Ambanis it gave them the protection from any of their competitors and enemies.

The transformation was best captured by *Business Today* in its sixth anniversary issue (1998) on India's Business Families: 'From scale to integration, from operational efficiencies to financial management, RIL represents the best of India Inc. As it witnesses dramatic increase in size, RIL's sina qua non status will only be accentuated. But where does it go from here? While RIL claims that its future lies only at home, it has already reached a stage where its pre-eminence is unquestionable. On that basis, RIL will have to look outwards to compete with DuPont, Dow Chemicals, Mitsui and Monsanto. It will also have to constantly re-invent itself to larger scales besides presenting a more transparent organization. Says Anil: "RIL will have to ensure that it remains more than a mere global company." If the Brothers Ambani believe that, then the transnationalization of RIL is inevitable in the next fifty – nay, five – years.' How ironical that seven years after this piece, Reliance has split and will find it difficult to achieve the heights that *Business Today* predicted in 1998.

However, one needs to still answer a few questions: what really were the secrets behind Dhirubhai's ability to ward off all challenges? What did he have that others didn't? How did he manage to reach heights that one can only dream about?

Probably his best trait was a sixth sense to visualize the future – both at micro and macro levels. For instance, he knew at some stage that the future lay in building large world-class plants that were cost-efficient, technologically modern and provided economies of scale due to huge capacities. He also knew instinctively that the future in communications was in being able to provide telecom services that would enable calls at the same rate as a postcard. His prediction is nearly coming out to be true.

I met Dhirubhai the first time outside the finance secretary's office – in the finance ministry waiting lounge. Mukesh was with him and I had come with my boss during my first year in the profession. We got talking. For no apparent reason, Dhirubhai took off. He went into a long monologue about how India could wipe out Pakistan economically by changing its textiles-related policies. All that the country had to do was to encourage the polyester industry, make it world class, so that it could annihilate Pakistan's cotton textiles sector, which was its economic mainstay. It was an amazing talk. Here was an industrialist advocating policies that would help him the most. But he was garbing them in such a nationalistic manner that no one could really argue with him on his objectives. No one could say he was being selfish. That was the quintessential Dhirubhai – a man with ideas, a man with vision, a man who would stop at nothing.

Another outstanding quality was to build loyalty and trust – both inside his organization and outside. When he ventured into business, he offered jobs to relatives, friends and colleagues from India and Aden. And those who remained loyal to him were taken good care of, even after they had retired. This policy even included outsiders (in media, politics, bureaucracy or elsewhere) who had helped Dhirubhai or Reliance. Even his millions of investors felt that Dhirubhai would never let them down; he would always deliver results.

He also built an extremely efficient network that was adept at collecting information like a country's intelligence agency. No information was taboo – whether it was about business, politics or sheer gossip. Dhirubhai never depended on one, two or three sources for information. Everyone who was useful was hired – on a permanent, temporary or no basis. And the sources could be unrelated; they could be middlemen, journalists, politicians, bureaucrats, PSU officials, lawyers, corporate honchos, socialites, and lobbyists. As long as they owed allegiance to the Ambanis, they were welcomed with open arms. All the information was funnelled to Dhirubhai and his two sons. At any given stage, they knew almost everything.

Another attribute of Dhirubhai was to leverage each strength and, in some cases, to find new ones. He realized that influx of equity capital could reduce the financial burden on his companies, that the conversion of debentures into shares could achieve the same objective and that it was easier to keep shareholders happy. Reliance's ability to think innovatively in this area was scintillating. Who could have thought that global investors would buy a 100-year bond issued by a mere corporate? Even some of the countries wouldn't be able to sell such long-term bonds. But RIL did it – and in style. As someone told me recently: 'Dhirubhai would never do anything that would harm his shareholders. He would have never done what his two sons did during the height of their public fight.'

Finally, Dhirubhai knew how to manage, influence, push, cajole, and force the policy environment. He would do anything to convince policy makers that his suggestions were worth their weight in gold. He had the intellectual base to converse with the knowledgeable, nationalistic phrases to woo the emotional, and forceful arguments to convert the non-believer. He once told a newsmagazine that one of his jobs was to get work done within the government. And he would salaam anyone to achieve that purpose. He had no ego about it. Recently, Arun Shourie, who was the worst enemy of Reliance in the 1980s and is now among the Ambani friends, praised Dhirubhai for his actions. Shourie felt that entrepreneurs like Dhirubhai expose the shallowness of restrictive policies by taking risks that ultimately help countries to grow. Therefore, according to Shourie, people like Ambani who push the envelope and probably drift on the wrong side of the law should actually be admired. Because, without such people, no country could ever grow dramatically. Without people like Dhirubhai, the nation could remain in a state of economic limbo with no pulls and pressures that can force policy makers and experts to rejig all mechanisms and systems.

8
The Future of Business Families

> *There is no instance of a nation benefiting from prolonged warfare.*
> — The Art of War by Sun Tzu
>
> *The whole idea of warfare is a fight unto death – for both the victor and the loser.*
> — Ambani interpretation

'Haveli ki umar saath saal,' said the late Pulin Garg, a professor in IIM, Ahmedabad. What he meant by that was that it was only natural for any business family to split, and that it normally took sixty years for this cycle to complete itself. Indeed, not too many business families remain by the time the third generation is ready to take over.

Within six decades, the grandchildren of the patriarch are ready to be inducted in business. By now, the joint family has become too large to accommodate so many inheritors with varying interests, characters, backgrounds and ambitions. Brij Mohan Munjal, the patriarch of the Ludhiana-based Hero group, where an informal division has already taken place, is a firm believer of the third generation factor. As he once told a business magazine, 'Once a family business crosses the third generation, it generally survives for many generations after that.' The Munjals exemplify this. Another example is that of the Tatas – although they benefitted because they had very few members in each generation. In fact, the Tatas epitomize, in some ways, how a family can remain intact despite horizontal and vertical growth of its empire.

In one of his columns, Gurcharan Das, former chief of P&G India, wrote: 'Thomas Mann, the Nobel Prize-winning German writer, expressed the same thoughts in his great novel *Buddenbrooks*, which is arguably the greatest book about a business family. It describes the saga of three generations: in the first generation the scruffy and astute patriarch works hard and makes money. Born into money, the second generation does not want more money. It wants power; it goes after it with the single-mindedness of a Joseph Kennedy, and Buddenbrooks' son becomes a senator. Born into money and power, what is left for the third generation to do but to dedicate itself to art? So the aesthetic but physically weak grandson plays the violin. But the signs of decline are visible and this is end of the Buddenbrooks family.'

Most family-owned business houses that came into being in the early part of the last century, were divided in the 1980s when the third generation was either already in business or just entering it. The decade witnessed corporate drama like none other, as it was the first time the splits happened in the public arena in full glare of the media. Whether it was the Birlas, headquartered in Kolkata and Mumbai, or the Delhi-based Shrirams, the divisions were forced by a string of third-generation scions who were rearing to run their own mini-empires and tread their individual corporate paths.

Obviously, the Birlas' was one of the most discussed splits. Not just because it was one of the largest business houses in India in 1986 when they officially broke up. But also because the family had so many high-profile members who tried all tactics to wring away whatever they could. However, G.D. Birla, the patriarch who presided over the division, ensured that it was done in a smooth manner. The story goes that all members sat around a table and patiently arrived at a consensus.

Almost all the Birla family members were successful entrepreneurs in their own right. Each of them was ambitious enough to feel that he could build a mega empire without the help of the others, or without having to stick with the others. Indeed, each had already proved his mettle. There was B.K. Birla and his son, the late Aditya Vikram, who were eyeing the top slot in Indian business. Both had grown their businesses in critical sectors like textiles (and fibres), cement and carbon black. In each area, they were among the leaders. K.K. Birla had made his name in textiles, sugar and media. M.P. Birla too was among the leaders in jute and cement. None of them wished to be saddled with the problems of being a part of a large family conglomerate that forces each group company to share the cash generated, sometimes to finance ventures by other family members. They wanted to use their individual cashflows to pursue their own dreams. Hence they split.

In a way, the Delhi-based Modi family, which was ruptured in the early 1990s, was also a third-generation split. After Gujar Mal Modi, the patriarch who built the empire in the first stage, died, his brother, K.N. Modi, took over the mantle. When the five sons of GM and the three of KN reached a certain age, they decided to slug it out publicly to get a larger slice of the business pie. This was a family battle that – like in the case of the Ambanis – was fought through the media. Obviously, politics and clout played an important part in deciding the winning faction, as we will see later in this chapter.

Unlike the cases of business families that were founded in the beginning of last century, those that were started in the second half of the century broke up much earlier. Here, it was the second generation that played a crucial role in effecting divisions. This is in keeping with worldwide trends. A study by the US life insurance firm, Mass Mutual, in the late 1990s concluded that 67 per cent of the family-owned businesses in the US split after the second generation took over, and this proportion increased to 90 per cent by the time the third generation came into the picture. The same is true about Indian families, although no conclusive study has been done on this aspect.

The splits in most neo-business families happened within a few decades of their existence – unlike the sixty years that was the benchmark in case of the older business families – as soon as the second-generation members had reached a respectable age of forty or so. Normally, an Indian family member assumes major control over the companies that he/she is managing at around the age of forty. In fact, there's a mystique attached to this age. Whether we look at the Ranbaxy group or the Nandas or the Thapars, the split happened within three to four decades of the patriarch setting up his group. And all the splits were initiated by second-generation members. They wanted to go their own ways – and had no qualms about splitting the group.

A study by Sudipt Dutta, who has written a book, *Business Families in India*, showed that 'the patriarch of the business usually ascends to his position around the age of forty. Like most things human, this is not an exact number, but a sample of ninety-one businessmen who are among the richest and the most prominent Indian businessmen shows that nearly 80 per cent of them came of age at around forty.

'The list is endless. Dhirubhai Ambani created Reliance as a brand when he was forty, as did Manu Chhabria embark on his spree of acquisitions; Aditya Birla made Grasim and Hindalco his centrepiece. A generation earlier, K.K. Birla shaped his fortunes around fertilizer; Sudarshan Birla made his most profitable forays into cement and chemicals; Nusli Wadia took his firm into chemicals and foods. This was equally true a generation earlier when J.R.D. Tata built up Telco. Similarly, the Wadias, or even Jamshed Tata, consolidated their main enterprise during these years. They had all been in business for a decade or more earlier but the inspiration to grow suddenly, spectacularly and successfully seems to be the product of their forties.'

The same theory probably held true for the patriarchs' sons and daughters who, at around forty, had this unbearable urge to spread their wings individually – and not as part of a joint business family or a close-knit empire.

The 1990s are replete with cases of businesses that split due to the second-generation factor. Bhai Mohan Singh's legacy was shared by his three sons – Parvinder

(Ranbaxy), Manjit (Montari Industries) and Analjit (Max India). L.M. Thapar, who himself was a product of a division within the Karam Chand Thapar group, gave way to the next generation – Vikram (Bilt), Gautam (Bilt Chemicals) and Karan (Greaves Cotton and Crompton Greaves). The mini-empire of the Campa Cola giant, Mohan Singh, was divided between Charanjeet (C.J. Hotels) and Daljeet (Pure Drinks). Even the newspaper baron Ramnath Goenka saw his empire being split up between Vivek Goenka and Manoj Sonthalia. Not to forget the rift between the two sons of H.P. Nanda, Rajan and Anil, in the Escorts group. While some of these divisions happened immediately after the death of the patriarch, others were effected while the founder was still alive. And, in most cases, the eldest sibling was in his/her forties!

Given this backdrop the Ambani feud was not surprising. It seemed inevitable – even in late 2002 – months after the death of the patriarch, Dhirubhai. It did not matter that the two sons, Mukesh and Anil, were publicly claiming that they were close to each other and could work together amicably. One knew it was a matter of when, not if. Not too many can stand up against the second-generation itch.

The questions still remain: Why do business families split so soon? Why doesn't the patriarch learn from the experiences of other families? Why can't siblings get along even for a few years after the patriarch's death? What centrifugal forces drive second generation members away?

One of the main reasons for this is that the founders invariably do not plan succession. For whatever reasons – either they believe in their own invincibility and ability to keep the flock together or have an overriding confidence in their offspring – they just do not think there could be a split in their family. It could happen to others, but not to them. The *Harvard Business Review* (May-June 1998) has quoted research on business families by the Arthur Andersen Center for Family Business, which co-sponsored a study with Mass Mutual's Family Business Enterprise.

Based on questionnaires completed by executives at 3000 family-run companies with sales of over $1 million, the study found that 53 per cent of these organizations expect their CEOs (owners) to retire within the next decade. 'And most of them have no succession plan in place of any sort. Consider too that only one-third of family-owned businesses survive a change in leadership. It's easy to see that many family businesses face a stormy future. "Many family businesses in America today are in a very fragile position," says Ross Nager, director of the Arthur Andersen Center for Family Business…'

Here's how the *HBR* described this phenomenon of a lack of succession planning. 'Forty- two per cent of the respondents reported that two or more family members may serve as co-CEOs in the next generation. Nager calls that a "notoriously fragile and difficult way to run a company"… Why do so few family businesses develop succession and strategic plans? Nager says the answer lies in the conflict business founders have always faced between being a fair parent and being a sound businessperson.

'"As a parent, a founder wants to treat the children equally, which means dividing the wealth equally," he says. "But the businessperson knows that the business should go to the most capable, qualified candidate." Often, the easiest solution is to ignore the conflict, never planning for the future. In addition, leaders of family businesses can be reluctant to retire because their identity is so tied up with the business. As a result, they either put retirement off indefinitely, or go into semi-retirement, creating an uncertain, unhealthy environment within the business.'

In the case of the Ambanis, the late Dhirubhai probably never believed that his two sons could fight so bitterly over the business spoils. But, at some level, he also realized that the real heir to his throne was the elder one, Mukesh. But he didn't wish to be 'unfair' to Anil. The two feelings together may have prompted him not to leave a will, and not to annoint a successor while he was still alive. L.M. Thapar, the second-generation owner of the Delhi-based Bilt group epitomizes the case of a businessperson who retired too late. The delay created unease and apprehension among the next generation members, especially because the inheritance in the group was unclear. LM never married and, therefore, had no children. But there were three young men – Gautam and Karan, who were sons of his sister, and Vikram, a cousin of theirs – hoping to take over LM's mantle. Finally, LM had no choice but to divide the group amongst them.

Another reason for the rift amongst the second generation is the question of sharing the booty. In some cases, there are cousins or nephews and nieces who feel they are being left out of the patriarch's wealth. This was a prominent factor that tore the Modis apart in the late 1980s and early 1990s. It was a tussle between the five sons of G.M. Modi and their three cousins, whose father, K.N. Modi, was the group chairman.

The trio felt that they were being forced to handle small businesses that had either no future or minimal cashflows. So, their ability to expand or diversify was limited. In comparison, GM's five sons managed the then cash cow, Modi Rubber (which made tyres), and other highly profitable ventures like Godfrey Philips and Modi Olivetti.

Events turned ugly when GM's five sons insisted that they were the real owners of the entire group. In those days, when I met B.K. Modi, who managed Modi Olivetti and part-managed Modi Rubber with his elder brother, he would categorically state that it was their father (GM) who built the group. GM's brother and BK's uncle, KN, always played second fiddle. After the patriarch's death, KN was just a titular group chairman, while GM's five sons handled all the important companies. So, explained BK, there was no chance that the group would be divided equitably among the eight claimants.

KN and his three sons retaliated with equal vigour. They said KN was always an equal partner to GM. That both had spent years in setting up the gigantic group. And this was adequately reflected in the various responsibilities that KN handled over decades. He was there at the shopfloor, construction sites of new factories and an active participant in key decision-making processes.

However, GM's five siblings did not want to give up control. For each was using Modi Rubber as the cash cow to grow their own individual empires. Eventually, the split happened but most of the group firms had been adversely affected by the power struggle. Today, the Modis are quite irrelevant as far as India Inc is concerned.

To better illustrate the issue of wealth in the context of the Indian business family, an example fleshed out by Sudipt Dutta should be enough. In 1999, he wrote that the secret behind the non-division of the Bajajs – it's a different matter that Bajaj Auto's Rahul Bajaj split with his brother Sishir only a few months ago – was due to the practice of socialism. A piece that Dutta wrote gave details of why he thought it was the key reason for the Bajajs to stay together, although a number of their family members were independently running companies and, therefore, had technically gone their separate ways.

'Neeraj, Rahul Bajaj's cousin, who runs Mukand Iron & Steel jointly with the sons of Viren Shah (who's married to Rahul's sister) and finds many financial advantages to a joint business family, attributes Bajaj's success in remaining together to the strict equality with which they divide the pie. "We may run businesses of different sizes but we have the same standard of living," says Neeraj Bajaj. "Rahul runs the Rs 2,500 crore Bajaj Auto and Shekhar (Rahul's another brother) runs the Rs 200 crore Bajaj Electricals, but they get equal salaries and equal pocket money. Splits take place when there is visible inequality. We take pains to observe absolute equality, and our fifteen rules keep us honest. We travel in the same type of cars; we are allowed the same class of air travel; we usually vacation together; thus, we minimise differences and comparisons.

'"Every year at Diwali, the family members get together and we review the fifteen rules by which we run our joint family. These rules relate to what each family member gets as pocket money, vacation allowance, what women spend on jewellery, and so on. Each year the family members update their allowances under the leadership of Rahul, who is presently the head of the household after my father Ramakrishna's death. And we meticulously stick to our pocket money. No exceptions! And I should know because I am currently the treasurer of the family, responsible for managing the family wealth, disbursing funds, filing tax returns and looking after the family affairs.'"

Despite modern tools, greater transparency and information overload, most business families are wracked by a general lack of communication. It may sound contradictory but, in reality, it is one of the foremost reasons for divisions and splits. For instance, it is clear that the two Ambani brothers were mostly outguessing the other's motive, without talking to each other directly. Information was filtering to them through their advisors, loyalists and friends – and the latter were interpreting and analysing it for the two scions. In the end, they thought each was trying to outsmart the other. If only they had talked, if only they had interacted regularly, a lot of their apprehensions could have been resolved behind closed doors without the entire world getting to know about their differences.

Similar problems were faced by most other families which couldn't stay together. Kimberly McCall, president of a business communications firm, once wrote that 'good communication practices don't come easily, but they can help or harm sibling relationship. It is not just establishing strong communication between family members, but creating a culture in which effective communication is an everyday practice. Most conflicts are the result of differing expectations and lack of communication. Messages are easily mixed – and when you have personal and business messages together, the chances are even higher for miscommunication.'

Leslie Dashew, a family-business authority in Atlanta who calls her consulting firm Human Side of Enterprise, has offered solutions to these issues. 'Bridging communication gap requires three major components. One is structure, consisting of channels, which could include councils, regular meetings and written communications such as newsletters and reports. Another is a safe environment in which people feel trusting enough to communicate freely. The third component consists of skills... which include the courage and confidence to overcome barriers...'

Communication should not simply be restricted to bare information about businesses, wealth, strategies, tactics and boardroom happenings. It should include discussion of emotional issues that regularly creep up between siblings or their spouses. The Ambani saga is full of such tensions between various characters, including those between the heirs apparent and their respective set of loyalists. So was the case with the Modis or the Chhabrias (who incidentally split within the first generation itself) or the Birlas. In fact, every business family – whether together or divided – has had its share of emotional tangles. These can also arise from the patriarch's own biases – he may like one sibling more than the other.

While tracking the Ambani fight, I was told time and again by people as to how the spouses of the two brothers had major roles to play in escalating the tensions. Yes, there were problems in business; but events within the Ambani residence had their own impact. Mukesh's wife Nita didn't like Tina's ostentatious show of wealth. Similarly, Anil's camp was upset with Nita's so-called arrogance.

As someone once said: 'Brother may meet brother with a smile, but make sure to bring along witnesses.' A member of a prominent Indian business family told Gurcharan Das that 'when things begin to sour, the family is the place where the most ridiculous and least respectable things in the world happen. People begin to take hints that were not intended and miss the hints that were intended. Family life is no longer an adventure, but an anxious discipline in which everybody is constantly graded for performance.'

Siblings or their spouses can also feel threatened and insecure vis-a-vis other members. This too leads to fissures that impact the businesses – finally leading to divisions. For example, the younger Chhabria brother, Kishore, always felt he was being forced to work under Manu's shadow. During the early 1990s, it was Manu who was being glorified by the media and the public for his breathtaking and scintillating string of takeovers and acquisitions. Manu was the visionary, strategist, takeover artist who was taking his Jumbo group to unbelievable heights. Kishore was always at the periphery, and never on the centrestage.

Finally, the inevitable happened when Kishore split with his brother in 1993. Worse, it seemed that the younger brother joined hands with Manu's arch enemy, the UB group's owner, Vijay Mallya. If that wasn't enough, Kishore fought an ugly legal-cum-corporate battle with Manu in a bid to wrest some brands and firms from the latter. The ugly battle dragged on for years. When the sky cleared over the Chhabria affair, Manu was no longer alive and his family had sold off most of the profitable Indian operations to different Indian groups, including that of Vijay Mallya.

It proved one point. As brothers Roger C. Allred and Richard S. Allred wrote in their book, *The Family Business: Power Tools for Survival, Success and Succession*: 'Family businesses have emotional issues, and they must be considered. Ignoring the passions that arise in a family business is like turning your back on a fire in your stockroom. You can ignore it for a while, but it will eventually destroy your business.' Business families across the world should take heed of this Chinese proverb: 'Govern a family as you would cook a small fish – very gently.'

Even if one can manage all the above issues – wealth sharing, communication gap, emotional mismatch – there's another factor that any patriarch or founder should take care of. This is about leaving behind a legacy of values. None described this better than Craig E. Arnoff, who holds the Dinos chair of Private Enterprise at Kennesaw State University, and John L. Ward, professor of Private Enterprise at Loyola University, in a piece they wrote in 1998.

'... as we have learned from so many exceptional family businesses, excellent financial returns are insufficient reason over the long-term for family-business cohesiveness and success. People are driven by more than money, and the efforts to assure family-business success require an abundance of heartfelt motivation. Successful business-owning families share explicit understandings of important mutual goals. These goals are often put into writing as a family mission statement or creed that explains what the family believes in and seeks together. The business is usually viewed as a means to achieve the family's goals...,' they said in the article.

'In the long run, our experience has taught us, the family cannot remain together and be harmonius if the motivation is only economic. In fact, increasing prosperity often weakens family bonds. The families that enjoy success through generations are often outstanding stewards as well as leaders. They realize outstanding long-term results on well-managed assets, but their primary motivation is to strengthen their families and give back to society. Owning a business together as a family can provide a great opportunity to achieve both purposes,' the two concluded.

Very few families have been able to do that – either in India or elsewhere – on a sustained basis and over a few generations. In an essay in 2003, author Gita Piramal examined the factors that enabled business families to survive and remain in the top 50 list on a consistent basis. She concluded that size mattered and that 'bigger family groups either take longer to wither away or are more resilient. Mumbai's shooting stars of the 1964-90 period, i.e., groups which dropped out of the ranking (Mangaldas Parekh, Scindia, Vissanji, Thackersey and Kilachand) are all from the bottom half of the list. Similarly, business families which dropped out of the list between 1990-99 (Chowgule, Mehra, Ghia, Ashok Birla and Nirlon) are also from the bottom half of the list... The list of survivors in this 35-year period is equally interesting: five of Mumbai's business groups (Tata, Birla, Bajaj, Mahindra and Wadia) appear to have taken huge changes in the competitive environment in their stride with remarkable dexterity.'

If what Piramal said is true, it would be logical to assume that business families that split had a lower chance of survival since the fragmented sub-groups would be much smaller than the original empire. Some, like the Shrirams, split numerous times leading to the formation of miniscule groups that slid down the ranking ladder and, finally, found it extremely difficult to survive. Size gives a business empire the necessary political, economic and financial clout; it also gives it the inherent strength to withstand cataclysmic changes due to competition, changing markets, or other factors.

In fact, this is exactly Piramal's second conclusion. 'Of the dropouts among Mumbai business houses between 1964-90, there have been family divorces in almost half the business groups: Thackersey, Kilachand, Ghia, Walchand, Khatau. Would they, could they, have remained in the top 50 league had they stayed together?' Other high profile, but recently splintered, Mumbai groups include those of Aditya Birla, Ajay Piramal, Harsh Mariwala, Rajen Raheja and Vijaypat Singhania. 'Would they, could they, have made it to the table had they not split up?' asks Piramal.

As mentioned earlier, most splintered groups have found it difficult to grow in size, while others have struggled to keep afloat. The Shrirams and the Modis were excellent examples of those who couldn't quite make it. In the DCM (Shrirams) group, one of the third generation members and a co-promoter of the car DCM-Daewoo, Vivek Bharat Ram, could not pay cash to buy shares he was entitled to in the rights issue meant to raise finances to expand the company's capacity. He was left with little choice but to become a minority partner (with just a 10 per cent stake) in DCM-Daewoo. The other brothers defaulted on interest and principal payments to banks and financial institutions and payments to depositors. Some of the members had no option but to divest unprofitable businesses as they did not have enough cashflows to expand capacity to gain economies of scale or invest in technology upgradation. The result: the mini-groups became smaller and smaller. Finally, they were on no one's radar.

However, splits in business families need not always mean bad news. As Dutta has said: 'Ironically, the recent family splits in India have helped to create (business) focus. When dividing assets the wiser families placed business interest over family interest and split their assets strategically. Thus, they ended up creating focused businesses, and they will gain major rewards from this virtuous decision. The majority though, divided their assets by placing family interest first; they split their assets in an illogical way with no synergy between divided companies.'

Look at what happened to the Bhai Mohan Singh family after the group was split between the three sons of the patriarch. Parvinder Singh got Ranbaxy, which was only into pharmaceuticals, and had no option but to focus his attention in that sector. Today, Ranbaxy is India's foremost pharma company and is recognized globally. Analjit got Max India, which was focused on telecom. But like an intelligent businessman, he took the bold decision that he couldn't be among the top three telecom players; so, he sold it at a huge profit and invested the cash in sunrise sectors like healthcare.

The Ambanis could go the same way. Post-split, Mukesh has a vertically integrated oil-petrochemicals-textiles conglomerate that can easily catapult itself into the list of top ten global energy firms. Anil could become a major player in the retail and services sector with telecom and power (where the retail segment is slowly being deregulated). Their future story could be that of Ranbaxy or of the Singhs.

Post Script: What I can say for sure is that whatever might happen to Indian family businesses – splits, divisions, fragmentation and, of course, competition because of the unleashing of economic reforms – they are here to stay. They might become smaller, they might lose their relevance, some of them could struggle, others might die, but their combined strength would still be relevant and critical for the country's economic growth. They would still play a pivotal role in making India an economic superpower.

Dwijendra Tripathi, an economic historian with enough knowledge of Indian business families, has supported this logic. First he contended that, contrary to common belief, the control of business families over their businesses or over a large chunk of Indian companies has actually grown since the 1950s. In that decade, most of Indian businesses – as opposed to those that were still owned by Britishers – were in the hands of eighteen families. Then came the series of family splits starting from the 1970s and escalating in the 1980s and the 1990s. But did that change anything? 'Despite loosening financial control over their companies and growing splits, the control of business families over the management of their concerns remains almost unimpaired,' said Tripathi.

Over 450 of India's most valuable companies are still family-owned. In fact, in the past decade or so, family members have increased their stakes in their group companies. Remember the 1970s and the 1980s when promoters would manage firms with a stake of 10 per cent, or even less. That was also the time when Swraj Paul, the NRI businessman based in the UK, launched hostile takeover raids on Escorts and DCM, where promoters' holdings were traditionally quite small.

All that changed with the onset of economic reforms in 1991. Owners realized that their firms would be under takeover threats in case they did not have substantial stakes in them. Ratan Tata, the head of the largest Indian group, was one of the many businessmen who saw the new threats. Using Tata Sons as the holding company, forcing cash-rich group companies to pump in money into Tata Sons by subscribing to its shares or debentures at huge premia, he raised enough corpus which was used to increase the family stakes in operational companies like Telco and Tisco. He also forced operational companies to invest in each other. In a sense, he created a tightly knit web that would make hostile takeovers of his group firms extremely difficult, if not impossible.

As the number of family-owned businesses grows in India, they can derive their confidence from just this one piece of statistic. 'Even in the US, the most professionalized business nation, 40 per cent of the GNP is still created by family companies and more than 80 per cent of all enterprises are family-run,' said Gurcharan Das. As a 1996 *Economist* piece noted: 'We forget that in most countries much of retail trade, small industry and all manner of services are in the hands of the family, from the corner store to the most high-tech manufacturing.'

9

Epilogue: End of an Era

After crossing a river, you should get far away from it.

— *The Art of War* by Sun Tzu

After crossing the bridge, you should go your separate ways that never intersect.

— Ambani interpretation

Finally, when it did happen, it came as no surprise. The division was along accepted lines – Mukesh got RIL and IPCL and Anil became the owner of RCIL, Reliance Infocomm, Reliance Energy and Reliance Capital.

Neither the family nor the RIL board members who went through the agreement over two days (17 and 18 June) gave further details. But we got a vague idea. Anil would be paid a cash compensation of Rs 4,500 crore; RIL would continue to provide guarantees that it had given on behalf of RCIL and Infocomm. RIL committed gas for Anil's proposed over Rs 10,000-crore power project in UP; there was a non-compete clause that was valid for five years; the future inheritance and destiny of the two sub-groups was decided as the children of the two brothers would manage the respective businesses.

After the deed was done, there were emotional outbursts – all of them planned and deliberate. The credit for solving the Reliance crisis went to the mother, Kokilaben. In front of TV cameras, Anil expressed his gratitude to the mother and also his two sisters. He also wished his elder brother luck and confidently predicted that RIL would do better in the future. The Reliance board got into the act too. In a press statement issued the same day, the board of directors 'placed their deep appreciation of the sincere and painstaking efforts taken by Smt. Kokilaben Ambani in working towards the settlement that will further enhance the value of the Reliance group. The Board further expressed their gratitude to Smt. Kokilaben Ambani for finding an amicable solution in the overall interests of the company...'

The media too went overboard. In her column in *The Times of India* (26 June 2005), Shobhaa De called Kokilaben 'Mother India.' Even the conservative *India Today* titled its cover story on the settlement as 'Mother Power'. It's author, Prabhu Chawla, wrote: 'On that Saturday morning, when the brothers were disarmed at her command, she was more than a mother. She was the matron saint of partitioned peace and sole protector of the indivisible legend of Ambani... On 16 June, she issued the ultimatum: nobody would leave the room without a final document of truce in place. After thirty-four hours, there was one, agreed upon by all, that spelt out the partition, the valuation and the road map. On the morning of 18 June, when Kokilaben announced the bittersweet news of an *Empire Divided*, it was Mother's Day in the hoary history of the Ambanis.'

Kokilaben herself was at the forefront to acknowledge that she was the one behind the agreement between her two sons. In fact, the first press release on 18 June was a statement by the mother. Issued on her letterhead – with an Om emblem on the top, the statement read: 'With the blessings of Srinathji (the family deity), I have today amicably resolved the issues between my two sons, Mukesh and Anil, keeping in mind the proud legacy of my husband, Dhirubhai Ambani...'

Wading through the morass of press releases, personal statements, media columns and cover pieces, I was struck by a number of niggling issues. It was, however, impossible to get any answers from the players – they just refused to say anything beyond what they had. A spokesperson for Mukesh told me that none of them would talk until the entire process was over, that is, until the legal and other formalities had been completed. That could take months. Anil's advisors too did not wish to say anything. One of them was holidaying in the US and said he couldn't comment; the other refused to take my calls.

The mother, of course, had never met journalists or discussed anything in public. Her life revolved around talking to her sons, the mediators and the various gurus that she visited regularly. (In fact, the story goes that one of the gurus told her that if the patch-up between her sons was delayed beyond 6 July – Dhirubhai's death anniversary – it would take months, or even years, before it could be resolved. That's why Kokilaben was interested that an agreement should be reached before that date.)

I was intrigued by Kokilaben's role in the entire issue. Her statement that she was responsible for the agreement sounded a bit strange. She could have easily stopped at saying, I am happy and pleased that my two sons have reached an agreement. Why did she have to tell the world about her involvement? It was just so unlike Kokilaben, who had always been publicity-shy. So why go to the other extreme? I think there was a specific reason for doing so.

Her statement was meant to send a message that an internal problem had been sorted out within the family. While outsiders – like Kamath, Kampani and others – had helped in the peace process, it was the eldest family member who was really responsible for the rapprochement between the two brothers. In a sense, it told everyone that, at the end of the day, the Ambanis remained a happy family.

My hunch is that Kokilaben was not even seriously involved in the entire peace process. She may have set some benchmarks – simple ones like telling her sons to resolve the issue fast and not go on washing dirty linen in public, or to cajole them to talk peace and not war – but that's about it. I started thinking along these lines after I was constantly told by Anil's advisors that Kokilaben was involved at every step of the feud. 'Anil discusses all his moves with her; she knew about all the revelations about Infocomm and other issues,' said one of them. One day, in January 2005, when I was discussing the 28 December 2004 meeting of the family to finalize the settlement (which was proven false), an Anil aide said: 'Anil disclosed the details of the December meeting only because his mother wanted him to do so. She wanted everyone to know the details so that Mukesh wouldn't be able to deny them later. It was her idea, not Anil's. She forced him to do so.'

Why would Anil's advisors go on and on about the mother? Going by what normally happened in traditional Gujarati families, the mother and the two sisters (Nina and Dipti) would play quite an insignificant role in the entire settlement process. I could understand Mukesh and Anil going public – as they did in December 2004 and January 2005 – that they had left it to the mother to sort out their differences, but I could not imagine it happening in real life. And, as events proved (see Chapter 6), the final discussions were between the mediators and loyalists on both sides, and also between the two brothers in the last stage. The fact is that the mother probably would not have even understood the complicated details about the split and the division.

In fact, it was Anil who told his friends in January 2005 that his mother only wished for a 'fair' settlement. 'She is a conservative woman who reads magazines like *Chitralekha* and doesn't understand business. So, she has left it to us but she wants things to be settled fast,' he explained. Now, suddenly, everyone – including Kokilaben – was shouting from the rooftops that she was responsible for the amicable division between her two sons!

I was also amazed by the word 'amicable.' What was amicable about the whole affair? For months, the two brothers hurled mud at each other, some of which stuck. For months, they ripped apart each other's credibility as entrepreneurs. For months, they exposed the unprofessional manner in which each ran his companies. They told the public that Reliance was neither professionally managed nor had world-class standards. They exposed the alleged dishonesty of seniormost managers in the group. They attacked, savaged, and injured each other. They lied, spoke half-truths, and manipulated the media, employees and the 3.5 million shareholders. Suddenly, they were talking of an amicable solution!

At another level, I was also appalled by the two statements issued by the RIL board on 18 June. To make things clear, we are talking about a board that comprised professionals, of directors who managed India's largest private sector company, of people who ran a professional and global-sized firm, of those whose first priority should be to further the interests of their shareholders. But, for seven months – or even before – they had just kept quiet. Even when they said anything, they only took Mukesh's side. And now, they were using reverential words for a member of the promoter family who had earlier never played any role in taking decisions that impacted RIL's business or its future. They were literally going down on their knees to acknowledge Kokilaben – not once but twice on the same day.

Whatever may be their reasons, it told me one thing about Reliance. The most loved, the most hated, the most revered and the most respected Indian group would never be the same again. It had lost a lot of its sheen and glamour and it would take a long time for both Mukesh and Anil to regain Reliance's earlier glory. The matters were made worse because, despite the division, the two brothers had still to reconcile with what had happened in the last seven months – between November 2004 and June 2005. Those events would continue to haunt them for a long time to come.

I recognized this when I heard a lot of FoMs (Friends of Mukesh) saying that Mukesh was unlikely to ever forget the manner in which his younger brother had tried to malign his character. They were unanimous in their conviction that the elder brother would extract his revenge – some day, even if he had to wait for years. 'In that sense, he's just like his father – never forgive an enemy and never forget a friend,' said one of his Mumbai-based corporate friends. Another one felt that Mukesh would do anything to make Anil's life hell, especially as a businessman.

As I see it, Mukesh has several opportunities to do that. RIL, now owned by Mukesh, has promised gas for Anil's proposed power project. But the price of the gas hasn't been decided. What if Mukesh asks for a really high price? It can make Anil's plan unviable from Day One. If Anil then has to seek other sources, it can still make his project unworkable. One option is to use LNG (liquified natural gas) as fuel, but its global prices are much higher than natural gas from domestic sources. In addition, Anil will either have to spend money on building a LNG re-gassification terminal – LNG is shipped at extremely cold temperature and needs to be re-gassified to be used as fuel — or pay the supplier an additional amount.

Anil can also source gas from other domestic sources – Cairns has recently struck gas in Rajasthan's Barmer district. But those fields have much smaller reserves. Or Anil can negotiate supply agreements with neighbouring nations like Bangladesh or Myanmar, which are keen to supply gas to Indian users. But then the younger Ambani will have to deal with political and diplomatic bottlenecks taking into account the current delicate – with more downs than ups – relations that New Delhi has with Dhaka, and the negative global pressures that New Delhi can face if it cozies up to Yangon. So the best option for Anil is to negotiate an attractive supply agreement with RIL. The question is, Will Mukesh agree, given what Anil has done to him?

Mukesh can squeeze Anil on Reliance Infocomm, which hangs over both brothers like a Damocles sword. As mentioned in Chapter 6, Infocomm's future will continue to depend on RIL, which has a huge financial stake in the telecom venture. Mukesh can always pull these levers to harm Infocomm. Add to that the fact that Anil will find himself in the hot seat at regular intervals due to Infocomm. The younger brother will be stuck with Infocomm's legal imbroglio (the case against its call re-routing issue is still pending in the Supreme Court), as well as the firm's bloated accumulated losses and non-receivables of Rs 3,500 crore. (Infocomm did earn a meagre profit in 2004-05, but incurred huge losses before that and it was Anil who blew the lid on the non-receivables, as explained in Chapter 4.) So, if he faces additional pressure due to Mukesh, Anil can sink with Infocomm.

Ironically, Infocomm, despite going to Anil, still has the potential to harm Mukesh. Before the deal with his brother on 18 June, Mukesh managed the telecom business and, therefore, he will be responsible for any past acts of ommission and commission. Worst among these will be the court's ruling on allegations pertaining to re-routing of international calls as local ones. In the recent past (see Chapter 6), internal Reliance e-mails have surfaced that have highlighted the role of Manoj Modi, a close Mukesh ally, in pushing through this scheme that has been deemed illegal by both the telecom ministry and the DoT. Days before the brothers announced their truce, more e-mails were sent anonymously to journalists.

Although the veracity of these new e-mails haven't been established, they reveal that Modi was very much involved in managing the re-routing crisis. Apparently, he had also convinced officials in Bharat Sanchar Nigam Ltd., the government-owned telecom service provider, that re-routing did not violate either the spirit or the letter of the existing laws. Some of these e-mails hinted at political-corporate corruption in a bid to get the government off Reliance's back on this issue. Security agencies like the CBI and the IB are also snapping at Reliance's heels as the re-routing might have violated the country's security ambit. Therefore, Modi – and hence, Mukesh – would continue to find themsleves in the dock until the court judgment.

Thanks to this ongoing controversy, Mukesh will be under pressure to distance himself from loyalists like Modi and Anand Jain, who is seen by many friends – and especially by Anil – as the villain of the entire Ambani affair. Days after the Ambani truce, there were reports in the media that Anand Jain had been removed as a director of IPCL, a company that has landed in Mukesh's fold. A spokesperson for Mukesh dismissed this, but a keen Ambani watcher told me: 'Mukesh put his foot down and didn't do it. In that sense, he's like his father – if he's forced or coerced to do something, he'll fight back and not do it. He'll only do what he wants to do of his own free will.'

Still, Mukesh will have to deal with his proximity to Anand Jain as the rest of his family seems to have cut off ties with him (no one, except Mukesh and Nita, attended the marriage of Jain's daughter, held in Goa the day the Ambanis announced the division. Even the reception in Mumbai saw the absence of most members.)

For Anil, the pressure points will be different. Apart from Infocomm's inherent problems and Mukesh's ability to tighten the screws against him, and despite the huge cash compensation that he will get, he will need to keep sinking in money in all his ventures, which are cash-guzzlers. As pointed out in earlier chapters, the telecom venture requires thousands of crores of rupees in the next few years. Money will have to be found to finance the promoter's equity of the UP power project. Even Reliance Capital will need huge amounts, if Anil has to brighten its future by making it a one-stop financial superstore. Anil is already talking of Reliance Capital's expansion into banking – which will require substantial investments – and the proposed buy-back of its shares that will entail an expenditure of nearly Rs 2,000 crore. Anil plans to raise huge resources from the open market, but it could saddle his firms with either huge debts or slightly bloated equity. The only advantage: Anil has been the master of raising resources for the Reliance group; but then he had the cash-cow's (RIL) equity behind him. Those old rules may not apply in the new environment.

At the same time, Anil will be a man in a hurry. In the past, he has been criticized for his inability to set up factories, units or projects. He has always managed what he has got on a platter – be it Reliance Energy or some facets of RIL. He now has to prove that he's also an entrepreneur in his own right – just like his elder brother, who has proved himself by building mega projects. Therefore, Anil will need to take fast decisions; but in his haste, he may make mistakes.

Mukesh could also falter. He will now try and make his part of the empire as large as he had originally planned. Before the Ambani spat and the subsequent split, Mukesh was keen to make his group the largest in the country. Apart from growing RIL into a Rs 100,000-crore company in the next few years, he thought Infocomm would provide the platform to increase the group turnover to, maybe, about Rs 150,000 crore in the same period. Then, Reliance had the ambitious foray into retail of petroleum products – through hundreds of petrol pumps – which could further hike the figure towards the Rs 200,000 crore mark. That would have made it, by far, the largest group in India and one of the largest in the world.

Things have obviously changed now. With Infocomm gone, Mukesh may be forced to aggressively look at other areas. For one, he will try to shorten the time period for expansion into petroleum retail outlets. RIL has also talked about entering the conventional retail sector – it wants to become India's Wal-Mart by setting up dozens of malls and also getting into other real estate-related areas. The mall project itself is estimated to cost upwards of Rs 1,000 crore over the next few years. Indications are that Reliance will venture into a few sectors that do not fit in with its core competence. So there's a risk that Mukesh could err in his business judgment.

Both Mukesh and Anil would need to confront rising competition in their respective sectors. Until now, RIL was the king of petrochemicals. There wasn't any Indian firm that could even dream of becoming that huge in this sector. Not any more. Meet Purnendu Chatterjee, the New York-based chairman of The Chatterjee Group (TCG) and the brain behind Haldia Petrochemicals that he set up in West Bengal and turned around its fortunes after years of teething problems. In May 2005, Purnendu struck a deal of a lifetime – by Indian standards, it was the corporate deal of the century, bigger than any clocked by an Indian, NRI or even those with foreign citizenships. He teamed up with another daring risk-taker, the Russian-born billionaire and owner of Access Industries, Leonard Blavatnik, to buy Basell, the world's largest producer of polypropylene (a key raw material to make certain petrochemicals and plastics), for a whopping $5.7 billion. It immediately catapulted Chatterjee into the big league.

Clearly, the Chatterjee-Blavatnik combine – their ambition is to dominate the global petrochemicals market — could take on RIL and Mukesh. Anil would also have to fight similar market duels, especially in telecom. The UPA government has increased foreign direct investment cap in the telecom sector – from 49 per cent to 74 per cent. Experts feel that this would attract fresh foreign investments, at least in two existing firms, Airtel (owned by Sunil Mittal) and Hutch. SingTel, the Singapore-based firm that owns a substantial chunk in Mittal's telecom venture, has already announced that it would wish to increase its stakes in existing ventures in Asia. Hutch too would want to pump in more money to expand its services in India. Both these foreign firms have deeper pockets than Reliance Infocomm. And both provide cellular services on a different platform – GSM, as opposed to Infocomm's CDMA technology. Ultimately, the fight in the Indian market – contrary to most other markets where only one of these technologies exist – will be about which one will hold more sway. It would be a marketing battle requiring huge investments. Anil would have to think of how to raise resources to counter moves from the two foreign firms.

There was a fight. Then there was truce. Finally, a deal was inked by Mukesh and Anil to divide the Reliance empire and go their separate ways. For many, it would seem like the end of an era in the long, exciting, adventurous and controversial history of the Ambani family. But, as I have explained above, the final chapter is yet to be written in this saga. There's more to watch out for – both to witness the progress made by each brother and to gauge whether their paths would cross in other messy ways along that route. However, as far as I am concerned, this is the end of my immediate tryst with the House of Ambanis.

Roli/398/22/6/06